# Better Homes and Gardens®

Homemade Cookies

Our seal assures you that every recipe in *Homemade Cookies*
has been tested in the Better Homes and Gardens® Test Kitchen.
This means that each recipe is practical and reliable, and
meets our high standards of taste appeal.

**HOMEMADE COOKIES**
Editor: Mary Jo Plutt
Editorial Project Manager: Rosanne Weber Mattson
Graphic Designer: Mary Schlueter Bendgen
Electronic Text Processor: Joyce Wasson
Food Stylists: Janet Herwig
Contributing Food Stylists: Kathleen E. German, Pat Godsted
Contributing Photographers: Scott Little; Shigeta Associates, Inc.

**On the front cover:** Red Raspberry Twirls and Brown
Sugar Slices (see recipes, page 45)

If you're a cookie-holic like I am, you're always looking for more cookie recipes. In Better Homes and Gardens® *Homemade Cookies*, I've included some favorite traditional cookie recipes along with some new ideas. For example, if you love those big, chewy cookies from cookie shops, try our Gourmet Cookies on page 7. You'll find them just as delicious, if not better! Or, if you're a brownie lover, try the seven-in-one brownie recipes on pages 24–28. I've taken a basic brownie and turned it into Candy-Topped Brownies, Cheesecake Brownies, and Nutty Caramel-Topped Brownies, to name a few.

And, of course, no cookie book would be complete without including some recipes for the holidays. Our chapter of "No-Fuss Festive Cookies" is a special one for me, and I hope for you. It's designed to give even the busiest cook a chance to bake during the hectic holidays. You'll find these cookies are every bit as decorative as traditional holiday cookies, but they're quicker and easier to make.

So come on, choose from our brand-new treasury of cookie recipes. I guarantee you won't be disappointed.

Mary

# Contents

# Cookie Jar Favorites

Here you'll find all kinds of cookies—drop, sliced,
shaped, cutout, and bar cookies. Indulge
in old-fashioned, family-style *Chocolate Chip Cookies* or
*Peanut Butter Crisscrosses*. Or, discover a new recipe
like *Gourmet Cookies* or *Lemon Poppy Seed Slices*. What-
ever your baking pleasure, we're confident you
and your family will find our scrumptious collection
of recipes irresistible.

# Cookie Basics

## Cookie-Baking Hints

Cookie baking—it's easy, fun, *and* best of all, it's delicious. As you bake your way through our special selection of cookie recipes, here are some quick tips from our Test Kitchen for successful cookies.

● Measure all of the ingredients accurately. Use glass measuring cups for liquid ingredients and dry measuring cups for dry ingredients.

● Save time by skipping the traditional step of beating the sugar and margarine, butter, or shortening together in a separate bowl from the dry ingredients. Our cookie recipes have been tested to allow you to add all the ingredients to a bowl, then mix. We think this new method gives you the same great taste with less work.

● If using a portable mixer, stir in by hand the last of the flour.

● To quickly firm up doughs for easier handling, form the dough into a flat loaf. Cover and place the dough in the freezer for *one-third* the time you would normally refrigerate it.

● Avoid using dark cookie sheets, because they absorb heat and may cause overbrowning on the bottoms of cookies. Shiny, heavy-gauge aluminum sheets work well, and so do nonstick cookie sheets if they're not too dark.

● Preheat oven about 10 minutes before baking.

● Grease cookie sheets *only* when the recipe recommends it. Otherwise, the cookies may spread too much.

● Always place cookie dough on cool cookie sheets to keep it from spreading.

● Bake cookies on the middle oven rack for even baking.

● Check cookies for doneness at the minimum baking time given in each recipe. Use a timer to avoid guesswork.

● Remove cookies from cookie sheets immediately unless otherwise directed.

● Cool cookies on a rack for even cooling. Wire racks are best because they can be washed easily. Wooden racks may get spotted from the oils in the cookies.

## All About Margarines

The firmness of cookies varies, depending on the type of margarine you use. Margarine that's made from 100 percent corn oil makes cookie dough so soft that, in some cases, added chilling time is needed.

Drop and bar cookies made with 100 percent corn oil won't need any chilling. Cutout cookies will require at least 5 hours of chilling time before you roll out the dough. And for slice-and-bake cookies, chill the rolls of dough in the freezer rather than in the refrigerator.

Avoid using products labeled "spreads" and "diet" because they won't produce a workable dough. Also, avoid soft-style tub products because they have a high percentage of air whipped into them.

# Drop Cookies

*So easy to make—just drop spoonfuls of dough onto the cookie sheet.*

## Ranger Cookies

*Full of cereal, coconut, and dates for extra goodness.*

½ cup margarine *or* butter
1¼ cups all-purpose flour
½ cup sugar
½ cup packed brown sugar
1 egg
1 teaspoon vanilla
½ teaspoon baking powder
¼ teaspoon baking soda
2 cups crisp rice cereal
    *or* 1 cup rolled oats
1 3½-ounce can (1⅓ cups)
    flaked coconut
1 cup pitted whole dates,
    snipped, *or* raisins

● In a mixing bowl beat margarine or butter with an electric mixer on medium to high speed about 30 seconds or till softened. Add about *half* of the flour, the sugar, brown sugar, egg, vanilla, baking powder, and baking soda. Beat till thoroughly combined. Then beat or stir in the remaining flour. Stir in cereal or oats, coconut, and dates or raisins.

● Drop dough from a rounded teaspoon 2 inches apart on an ungreased cookie sheet. Bake in a 375° oven about 8 minutes or till lightly browned. Cool on cookie sheet for 1 minute. Then remove cookies and cool on a wire rack. Makes about 54.

Nutrition information per cookie: 63 calories, 1 g protein, 10 g carbohydrate, 2 g fat, 5 mg cholesterol, 43 mg sodium, 40 mg potassium.

## Gourmet Cookies

*They're just like cookies from a cookie shop—big, chewy, and filled with lots of chocolate chunks and nuts.*

2 cups rolled oats
¾ cup margarine *or* butter
¾ cup sugar
¾ cup packed brown sugar
2 eggs
1 teaspoon baking soda
1 teaspoon vanilla
1 cup all-purpose flour
1 12-ounce bar milk
    chocolate *or* 12 ounces
    white baking bar with
    cocoa butter, cut into
    ½-inch pieces
1 cup coarsely chopped
    macadamia nuts,
    walnuts, *or* pecans

● For oat flour, in a blender container place *½ cup* oats. Cover and blend till oats turn into a powder. Transfer powder to a small bowl. Repeat with remaining oats, using ½ cup at a time.

● In a mixing bowl beat margarine or butter with an electric mixer on medium to high speed about 30 seconds or till margarine or butter is softened. Add the oat flour, sugar, brown sugar, eggs, baking soda, and vanilla. Beat till combined, scraping sides of bowl occasionally. Beat or stir in all-purpose flour. Stir in chocolate or baking bar pieces and nuts.

● Drop *¼ cup* of dough at a time 4 inches apart on an ungreased cookie sheet. Bake in a 350° oven for 13 to 15 minutes or till edges are golden. Cool on cookie sheet for 1 minute. Then remove the cookies and cool on a wire rack. Makes about 18.

Nutrition information per cookie: 350 calories, 5 g protein, 40 g carbohydrate, 20 g fat, 34 mg cholesterol, 179 mg sodium, 179 mg potassium.

# Basic Drop Cookies

*Here you'll find seven drop-cookie recipes in one. For plain cookies, bake the Basic Drop Cookies; for fancier ones, try any of the six variations on pages 10 and 11.*

½ cup shortening
½ cup margarine *or* butter
2¼ cups flour
¾ cup sugar
¾ cup packed brown sugar
2 eggs
1 teaspoon baking soda
1 teaspoon vanilla

● In a mixing bowl beat shortening and margarine or butter with an electric mixer on medium to high speed about 30 seconds or till softened.
● Add about *half* of the flour, the sugar, brown sugar, eggs, baking soda, and vanilla to shortening mixture. Beat till combined. Beat or stir in remaining flour.
● Drop dough from a rounded teaspoon 2 inches apart on an ungreased cookie sheet. Bake in a 375° oven for 8 to 10 minutes or till edges are golden. Cool on cookie sheet for 1 minute. Then remove cookies and cool on a wire rack. Makes about 48.

Nutrition information per cookie: 85 calories, 1 g protein, 4 g fat, 11 g carbohydrate, 11 mg cholesterol, 50 mg sodium, 21 mg potassium.

Hazelnut-Date
Cookies

Banana Nut
Cookies

Carrot Cake
Cookies

Chocolate Chip
Cookies

Double-Chocolate
Chunk Cookies

Basic Drop
Cookies

Oatmeal-Raisin
Cookies

9

## Chocolate Chip Cookies

*For Chocolate Chip Bars: Spread the dough into an ungreased 15x10x1-inch baking pan; bake in a 350° oven for 20 to 25 minutes. (Cookies are pictured on pages 8–9.)*

1 **recipe Basic Drop Cookies (see page 8)**
1 12-ounce package (2 cups) semisweet chocolate *or* butterscotch-flavored pieces
1 cup chopped walnuts *or* pecans

● Prepare dough for Basic Drop Cookies as directed, *except* after mixing in the last of the flour, stir in the chocolate or butterscotch-flavored pieces and walnuts or pecans. Bake and cool as directed. Makes about 60.

Nutrition information per cookie: 110 calories, 1 g protein, 12 g carbohydrate, 7 g fat, 9 mg cholesterol, 40 mg sodium, 45 mg potassium.

## Carrot Cake Cookies

*Need to feed a crowd? Try these bite-size carrot cakes. (Pictured on pages 8–9.)*

1 **recipe Basic Drop Cookies (see page 8)**
1 teaspoon ground cinnamon
1 cup coarsely shredded carrot
½ cup coconut
½ cup chopped walnuts
½ cup well-drained crushed pineapple
   Cream Cheese Frosting

● Prepare dough for Basic Drop Cookies as directed, *except* mix in cinnamon with the sugar. Then after mixing in the last of the flour, stir in carrot, coconut, walnuts, and pineapple. Bake and cool as directed. Frost with Cream Cheese Frosting. Store cookies, covered, in the refrigerator. Makes about 72.

**Cream Cheese Frosting:** In a mixing bowl beat one 3-ounce package softened *cream cheese*, ¼ cup softened *margarine* or *butter,* and 1 teaspoon *vanilla* till fluffy. Gradually beat in 2 cups sifted *powdered sugar* till smooth. Makes 1¼ cups.

Nutrition information per frosted cookie: 87 calories, 1 g protein, 11 g carbohydrate, 5 g fat, 9 mg cholesterol, 49 mg sodium, 29 mg potassium.

## Oatmeal-Raisin Cookies

*"Crispy on the outside and chewy on the inside" is how our Food Editors described these simple, old-fashioned favorites. (Pictured on pages 8–9.)*

1 **recipe Basic Drop Cookies (see page 8)**
½ teaspoon ground cinnamon
¼ teaspoon ground nutmeg
2 cups quick-cooking oats
1½ cup raisins *or* one 8-ounce package pitted whole dates, snipped

● Prepare dough for Basic Drop Cookies as directed, *except* reduce flour to *1½ cups* and mix in cinnamon and nutmeg with the sugar. Then after mixing in the last of the flour, stir in oats and raisins or dates. Bake and cool as directed. Makes about 60.

Nutrition information per cookie: 89 calories, 1 g protein, 13 g carbohydrate, 4 g fat, 9 mg cholesterol, 40 mg sodium, 54 mg potassium.

# Hazelnut-Date Cookies

*To trim these cookies, place whole nuts on top before baking. (Pictured on pages 8–9.)*

1 recipe Basic Drop Cookies
  (see page 8)
2 teaspoons finely shredded
  orange peel
1 tablespoon orange juice
1 cup (4 ounces) ground
  hazelnuts (filberts)
  *or* walnuts
1 cup coarsely chopped
  hazelnuts (filberts)
  *or* walnuts
1 8-ounce package chopped
  pitted dates

● Prepare dough for Basic Drop Cookies as directed, *except* reduce flour to *2 cups* and mix in the orange peel and juice with the sugar. Then, after mixing in the last of the flour, stir in ground and chopped nuts and dates. Bake and cool as directed. Makes about 66.

Nutrition information per cookie: 93 calories, 1 g protein, 11 g carbohydrate, 5 g fat, 8 mg cholesterol, 36 mg sodium, 54 mg potassium.

# Banana Nut Cookies

*They taste just like banana nut bread! (Pictured on pages 8–9.)*

1 recipe Basic Drop Cookies
  (see page 8)
1 cup mashed ripe banana
  (about 3 medium)
¼ teaspoon ground nutmeg
1 cup chopped walnuts

● Prepare dough for Basic Drop Cookies as directed, *except* mix in banana and nutmeg with sugar. Then, after mixing in the last of the flour, stir in walnuts. Bake and cool as directed, *except* use a lightly greased cookie sheet. Makes about 48.

Nutrition information per cookie: 105 calories, 1 g protein, 12 g carbohydrate, 6 g fat, 11 mg cholesterol, 50 mg sodium, 52 mg potassium.

# Double-Chocolate Chunk Cookies

*For Chocolate-Mint Chunk Cookies: Substitute 9 ounces of layered chocolate-mint wafers, chopped, for the white baking bar. (Pictured on pages 8–9.)*

1 recipe Basic Drop Cookies
  (see page 8)
2 squares (2 ounces)
  unsweetened chocolate,
  melted and cooled
1 9-ounce white baking bar
  with cocoa butter,
  coarsely chopped *or* one
  10-ounce package white
  baking pieces with cocoa
  butter (2 cups)

● Prepare dough for Basic Drop Cookies as directed, *except* mix in melted chocolate with the sugar. After mixing in the last of the flour, stir in white baking bar pieces.

● Drop dough from a rounded *tablespoon* 2½ inches apart on an ungreased cookie sheet. Bake in a 375° oven for 12 to 14 minutes or till tops look dry. Cool on cookie sheet for 1 minute. Then remove cookies and cool on a wire rack. Makes about 24.

Nutrition information per cookie: 240 calories, 3 g protein, 29 g carbohydrate, 13 g fat, 25 mg cholesterol, 109 mg sodium, 95 mg potassium.

# Peanutty Drop Cookies

*We stirred in both peanut butter and peanuts for an extra-nutty flavor. (Pictured on page 15.)*

½ cup margarine *or* butter
½ cup peanut butter
¼ cup shortening
2¼ cups flour
¾ cup sugar
¾ cup packed brown sugar
2 eggs
1 teaspoon baking soda
1 teaspoon vanilla
1½ cups chopped unsalted
   cocktail peanuts
   Whole unsalted cocktail
   peanuts (optional)

● In a mixing bowl beat margarine or butter, peanut butter, and shortening with an electric mixer on medium to high speed about 30 seconds or till softened.

● Add about *half* of the flour, the sugar, brown sugar, eggs, baking soda, and vanilla to the margarine mixture. Beat till thoroughly combined, scraping sides of bowl occasionally. Beat or stir in the remaining flour. Stir in chopped peanuts.

● Drop dough from a rounded teaspoon 2 inches apart on an ungreased cookie sheet. If desired, lightly press a few whole peanuts in center of each cookie. Bake in a 375° oven for 8 to 10 minutes or till edges are golden. Cool on cookie sheet for 1 minute. Remove cookies. Cool on a wire rack. Makes about 70.

Nutrition information per cookie: 81 calories, 2 g protein, 8 g carbohydrate, 5 g fat, 8 mg cholesterol, 43 mg sodium, 49 mg potassium.

# Toasted Sesame Seed Cookies

*Look for small containers of sesame seed in the spice section of the supermarket or buy it in bulk from a health food store.*

1 cup (5 ounces) sesame seed
¾ cups margarine *or* butter
2 cups all-purpose flour
1 cup packed brown sugar
2 eggs
1 teaspoon baking powder
1 teaspoon vanilla
½ teaspoon baking soda
¼ teaspoon ground ginger

● To toast sesame seed, place sesame seed in a large baking pan. Bake in a 350° oven for 10 to 15 minutes or till *lightly* browned, stirring after 7 minutes. Then set aside to cool.

● In a bowl beat margarine or butter with an electric mixer on medium to high speed about 30 seconds or till softened.

● Add about *half* of the flour, the brown sugar, eggs, baking powder, vanilla, baking soda, and ginger to the margarine. Beat till thoroughly combined, scraping sides of bowl occasionally. Beat or stir in the remaining flour. Stir in toasted sesame seed.

● Drop dough from a rounded teaspoon 2 inches apart on an ungreased cookie sheet. Bake in a 350° oven for 10 to 12 minutes or till edges are golden. Cool on cookie sheet for 1 minute. Then remove and cool on a wire rack. Makes about 48.

Nutrition information per cookie: 82 calories, 1 g protein, 9 g carbohydrate, 5 g fat, 11 mg cholesterol, 56 mg sodium, 39 mg potassium.

# Brown Sugar 'n' Spice Cookies

*Sugar 'n' spice—the name says it all.*

½ cup margarine *or* butter
1½ cups all-purpose flour
¾ cup packed brown sugar
¼ cup sugar
1 egg
1 teaspoon vanilla
½ teaspoon baking soda
½ teaspoon ground allspice
½ teaspoon ground cinnamon
½ cup chopped cashews
    *or* pecans
  Cashews *or* pecan halves
    (optional)

● In a bowl beat margarine or butter with an electric mixer on medium to high speed about 30 seconds or till softened.

● Add about *half* the flour, the brown sugar, sugar, egg, vanilla, baking soda, allspice, and cinnamon to the margarine. Beat till thoroughly combined, scraping sides of bowl occasionally. Then beat or stir in the remaining flour. Stir in chopped nuts.

● Drop dough from a rounded teaspoon 2 inches apart on an ungreased cookie sheet. Then slightly flatten with the tines of a fork. If desired, lightly press a nut in center of each cookie. Bake in a 375° oven for 8 to 10 minutes or till edges are golden. Cool on cookie sheet for 1 minute. Then remove cookies and cool on a wire rack. Makes about 36.

Nutrition information per cookie: 78 calories, 1 g protein, 11 g carbohydrate, 4 g fat, 8 mg cholesterol, 49 mg sodium, 36 mg potassium.

# Chocolate Peanut Crunch Cookies

*For extra peanut pizzazz, drizzle the cookies with Peanut Butter Frosting (see recipe, page 33).*

½ cup chunky peanut butter
⅓ cup margarine *or* butter
1 cup all-purpose flour
⅓ cup sugar
⅓ cup packed brown sugar
¼ cup chocolate-flavored
    syrup
1 egg
½ teaspoon baking soda
½ teaspoon vanilla

● In a mixing bowl beat peanut butter and margarine or butter with an electric mixer on medium to high speed about 30 seconds or till combined.

● Add about *half* of the flour, the sugar, brown sugar, chocolate-flavored syrup, egg, baking soda, and vanilla. Beat mixture till thoroughly combined, scraping sides of bowl occasionally. Then beat or stir in the remaining flour.

● Drop dough from a rounded teaspoon 2 inches apart on an ungreased cookie sheet. Bake in a 375° oven for 8 to 10 minutes or till tops look dry. Cool on cookie sheet for 1 minute. Then remove cookies and cool on a wire rack. Makes about 36.

Nutrition information per cookie: 71 calories, 2 g protein, 8 g carbohydrate, 4 g fat, 8 mg cholesterol, 56 mg sodium, 43 mg potassium.

# Pecan Drops

*Create glistening tops by sprinkling the cookies with a little bit of sugar just before baking.*

½ cup margarine *or* butter
2 cups sifted powdered sugar
1¾ cups all-purpose flour
⅓ cup milk
1 egg
1 teaspoon baking powder
1 teaspoon vanilla
1 cup coarsely chopped
   pecans
   Sugar
   Pecan halves (optional)

● In a bowl beat margarine or butter with an electric mixer on medium to high speed about 30 seconds or till softened.

● Add powdered sugar, about *half* of the flour, *half* of the milk, the egg, baking powder, and the vanilla to the margarine. Beat till thoroughly combined, scraping sides of bowl occasionally. Then beat or stir in remaining flour and milk. Stir in chopped pecans.

● Drop dough from a rounded teaspoon 2 inches apart on a greased cookie sheet. Sprinkle with sugar. If desired, lightly press a pecan half in center of each cookie. Bake in a 375° oven for 8 to 10 minutes or till edges are slightly golden. Remove cookies and cool on a wire rack. Makes about 36.

Nutrition information per cookie: 91 calories, 1 g protein, 11 g carbohydrate, 5 g fat, 6 mg cholesterol, 41 mg sodium, 24 mg potassium.

# Chocolate-Nut Cookies

*Forget the measuring. Start with a cake mix for a super-easy fudge cookie.*

1 package 1-layer-size
   devil's food cake mix
1 8-ounce carton dairy
   sour cream
½ cup peanut butter-flavored
   pieces *or* semisweet
   chocolate pieces
½ cup coarsely chopped
   walnuts

● In a mixing bowl beat cake mix and sour cream with an electric mixer on medium to high speed about 2 minutes or till smooth and creamy, scraping sides of bowl occasionally. Stir in peanut butter-flavored pieces or chocolate pieces and walnuts.

● Drop dough from a rounded teaspoon 2 inches apart on a greased cookie sheet. Bake in a 350° oven for 10 to 12 minutes or till tops look dry. Cool on cookie sheet for 1 minute. Then remove cookies and cool on a wire rack. Makes about 36.

Nutrition information per cookie: 66 calories, 2 g protein, 7 g carbohydrate, 4 g fat, 3 mg cholesterol, 42 mg sodium, 38 mg potassium.

Chocolate-Nut
Cookies

Peanutty Drop Cookies
(see recipe, page 12)

Pecan Drops

# Pumpkin Cookies

½ cup margarine *or* butter
1 cup all-purpose flour
1 cup packed brown sugar
1 cup canned pumpkin
1 egg
1 teaspoon ground cinnamon
1 teaspoon vanilla
½ teaspoon baking powder
½ teaspoon baking soda
½ teaspoon ground allspice
½ teaspoon ground nutmeg
¾ cup toasted wheat germ
1½ cup chopped walnuts
    *or* raisins

● In a bowl beat margarine or butter with an electric mixer on medium to high speed about 30 seconds or till softened.

● Add flour, brown sugar, pumpkin, egg, cinnamon, vanilla, baking powder, baking soda, allspice, and nutmeg to the margarine. Beat till thoroughly combined, scraping sides of bowl occasionally. Then beat or stir in wheat germ. Stir in walnuts or raisins. (Dough will be soft.)

● Drop dough from a rounded teaspoon 2 inches apart on a greased cookie sheet. Bake in a 375° oven for 8 to 10 minutes or till edges are firm. Remove cookies and cool on a wire rack. Makes about 48.

Nutrition information per cookie: 77 calories, 1 g protein, 8 g carbohydrate, 5 g fat, 6 mg cholesterol, 41 mg sodium, 65 mg potassium.

# Soft Ginger Cookies

½ teaspoon instant coffee
    crystals
½ cup margarine *or* butter
1½ cups all-purpose flour
½ cup sugar
¼ cup molasses
1 egg
1 teaspoon ground ginger
½ teaspoon baking soda
½ teaspoon ground cinnamon
¾ cup raisins *or* snipped
    dried apricots
    Coffee-Flavored Frosting

● In a custard cup stir together 2 tablespoons *hot water* and coffee crystals till dissolved. Set coffee mixture aside.

● In a bowl beat margarine or butter with an electric mixer on medium to high speed about 30 seconds or till softened.

● Add about *half* of the flour, the sugar, molasses, egg, ginger, baking soda, cinnamon, and coffee mixture to margarine. Beat till thoroughly combined, scraping sides of bowl occasionally. Beat or stir in the remaining flour. Stir in raisins or apricots.

● Drop dough from a rounded teaspoon 2 inches apart on a greased cookie sheet. Bake in a 350° oven for 8 to 10 minutes or till edges are firm. Remove cookies and cool on a wire rack. Frost cookies with Coffee-Flavored Frosting. Makes about 36.

**Coffee-Flavored Frosting:** In a small mixing bowl stir together 4 teaspoons *hot water* and ½ teaspoon *instant coffee crystals* till dissolved. Add 2 tablespoons softened *margarine* or *butter.* Gradually beat in 1½ to 1⅔ cups sifted *powdered sugar* to make frosting of spreading consistency. Makes ⅔ cup.

Nutrition information per frosted cookie: 91 calories, 1 g protein, 15 g carbohydrate, 3 g fat, 8 mg cholesterol, 56 mg sodium, 57 mg potassium.

# Delectable Prune Cookies

*Prunes in cookies? You bet! Use canned prune filling to make the job extra easy. Look for the product in the baking section of your supermarket.*

1 cup shortening
2 cups all-purpose flour
1 12-ounce can prune cake
    and pastry filling
1 cup sugar
2 eggs
1 teaspoon baking soda
1 teaspoon vanilla
½ teaspoon baking powder
½ teaspoon salt
2 cups quick-cooking
    rolled oats
2 cups crisp rice cereal

● In a mixing bowl beat shortening with an electric mixer on medium to high speed about 30 seconds or till softened.

● Add about *half* of the flour, the prune filling, sugar, eggs, baking soda, vanilla, baking powder, and salt to shortening. Beat till combined, scraping sides of bowl occasionally. Beat or stir in remaining flour. Stir in oats and cereal.

● Drop dough from a rounded teaspoon 1 inch apart on a lightly greased cookie sheet. Bake in a 350° oven for 10 to 12 minutes or till edges are golden. Remove cookies and cool on a wire rack. Makes about 84.

Nutrition information per cookie: 55 calories, 1 g protein, 7 g carbohydrate, 3 g fat, 7 mg cholesterol, 39 mg sodium, 12 mg potassium.

# Lemon Tea Cookies

*We call them "tea cookies" because they go so well with a cup of tea.*

1 teaspoon finely shredded
    lemon peel (set aside)
2 teaspoons lemon juice
⅓ cup milk
½ cup margarine *or* butter
1¾ cups all-purpose flour
¾ cup sugar
1 egg
1 teaspoon baking powder
¼ teaspoon baking soda
    Lemon Glaze

● In a glass measure stir lemon juice into milk, then let stand for 5 minutes.

● In a bowl beat margarine or butter with an electric mixer on medium to high speed about 30 seconds or till softened.

● Add about *half* of the flour, the sugar, egg, baking powder, baking soda, lemon peel, and milk mixture to the margarine. Beat till thoroughly combined, scraping the sides of bowl occasionally. Then beat or stir in the remaining flour.

● Drop dough from a rounded teaspoon 2 inches apart on an ungreased cookie sheet. Bake in a 350° oven for 10 to 12 minutes or till edges are lightly browned. Transfer cookies to a wire rack. Brush tops of warm cookies with Lemon Glaze, then cool. Makes about 48.

**Lemon Glaze:** In a small mixing bowl stir together ¼ cup *sugar* and 2 tablespoons *lemon juice.* Makes 3 tablespoons.

Nutrition information per glazed cookie: 52 calories, 1 g protein, 8 g carbohydrate, 2 g fat, 6 mg cholesterol, 37 mg sodium, 11 mg potassium.

# Peaches 'n' Cream Cookies

¾ cup finely snipped
dried peaches
¼ cup peach brandy, peach
schnapps, apricot nectar,
*or* orange juice
¾ cup margarine *or* butter
½ of an 8-ounce container
(½ cup) soft-style cream
cheese
1½ cups all-purpose flour
¾ cup sugar
1 egg
½ teaspoon baking powder
½ cup chopped walnuts
Peaches 'n' Cream Frosting

● In a small bowl stir together dried peaches and peach brandy, schnapps, apricot nectar, or orange juice. Let stand for 15 minutes. Then drain, reserving liquid for frosting.

● In a mixing bowl beat margarine or butter and cream cheese with an electric mixer on medium to high speed about 30 seconds or till softened.

● Add about *half* of the flour, the sugar, egg, and baking powder to margarine mixture. Beat till thoroughly combined. Then beat or stir in remaining flour. Stir in nuts and drained peaches.

● Drop dough from a *level tablespoon* 2 inches apart on an ungreased cookie sheet. Bake in a 350° oven for 10 to 12 minutes or till edges are golden. Remove cookies and cool on a wire rack. Frost cookies with Peaches 'n' Cream Frosting. Store, covered, in the refrigerator. Makes about 48.

**Peaches 'n' Cream Frosting:** In a medium mixing bowl beat 2 tablespoons *soft-style cream cheese,* 1 tablespoon *margarine* or *butter,* and *1 tablespoon* reserved liquid from peaches till light and fluffy. Gradually beat in 1½ cups sifted *powdered sugar.* If necessary, beat in an additional *1 to 2 teaspoons* reserved liquid to make frosting of spreading consistency. Makes ¾ cup.

Nutrition information per frosted cookie: 93 calories, 1 g protein, 11 g carbohydrate, 5 g fat, 6 mg cholesterol, 49 mg sodium, 30 mg potassium.

# No-Bake Cocoa-Oatmeal Cookies

2 cups sugar
¼ cup unsweetened cocoa
powder
½ cup milk
½ cup margarine *or* butter
1 tablespoon light corn syrup
¼ cup peanut butter
2 cups quick-cooking
rolled oats

● In a heavy saucepan stir together sugar and cocoa powder. Stir in milk. Add margarine or butter and corn syrup. Bring to boiling, stirring occasionally. Boil vigorously for 3 minutes.

● Stir peanut butter into mixture in saucepan till smooth. Then stir in rolled oats till well combined. Return mixture to boiling. Remove from heat. Using a wooden spoon, beat mixture till slightly thickened. Immediately drop mixture from a rounded teaspoon on a *waxed-paper-lined* cookie sheet. (If mixture spreads too much, beat it a little longer.) Cool. Makes about 36.

Nutrition information per cookie: 98 calories, 1 g protein, 15 g carbohydrate, 4 g fat, 0 mg cholesterol, 45 mg sodium, 39 mg potassium.

# Coconut Macaroons

*So light and airy you'll be floating on cloud nine with just one bite. (Pictured on page 20.)*

2 egg whites
½ teaspoon vanilla
⅔ cup sugar
1 3½-ounce can (1⅓ cups)
   flaked coconut

● In a large mixing bowl beat egg whites and vanilla with an electric mixer on medium speed till soft peaks form (tips curl). Gradually add sugar, beating till stiff peaks form (tips stand straight). Fold in coconut.

● Drop coconut mixture from a rounded teaspoon 2 inches apart on a greased cookie sheet. Bake in a 325° oven for 15 to 20 minutes or till edges are lightly browned. Remove cookies and cool on a wire rack. Makes about 30.

Nutrition information per cookie: 33 calories, 0 g protein, 6 g carbohydrate, 1 g fat, 0 mg cholesterol, 4 mg sodium, 14 mg potassium.

**Date 'n' Nut Macaroons:** Prepare Coconut Macaroons as directed above, *except* substitute ⅔ cup finely chopped pitted *dates* and ⅔ cup chopped *walnuts* for the coconut.

Nutrition information per cookie: 46 calories, 1 g protein, 8 g carbohydrate, 2 g fat, 0 mg cholesterol, 4 mg sodium, 42 mg potassium.

**Nutty Macaroons:** Prepare Coconut Macaroons as directed above, *except* fold in ½ cup chopped toasted *macadamia nuts, almonds, pecans,* or *hazelnuts (filberts)* with the coconut.

Nutrition information per cookie: 48 calories, 1 g protein, 6 g carbohydrate, 3 g fat, 0 mg cholesterol, 4 mg sodium, 22 mg potassium.

**Cereal 'n' Nut Macaroons:** Prepare Coconut Macaroons as directed above, *except* fold in 1½ cups *wheat flakes* and ½ cup chopped *walnuts* with the coconut.

Nutrition information per cookie: 49 calories, 1 g protein, 7 g carbohydrate, 2 g fat, 0 mg cholesterol, 18 mg sodium, 28 mg potassium.

**Currant Granola Mini-Bites**

**Apricot-Bran Drops**

**Coconut Macaroons**
(see recipe, page 19)

# Apricot-Bran Drops

*Test Kitchen Tip: To keep these tangy, cakelike cookies moist, store them in the freezer.*

¾ cup finely snipped,
    dried apricots
½ cup whole bran cereal
½ cup orange juice
½ cup margarine *or* butter
1½ cups all-purpose flour
½ cup sugar
½ cup packed brown sugar
1 egg
1 teaspoon baking powder
1 teaspoon vanilla
½ teaspoon ground cinnamon
⅓ cup chopped pecans
    Pecan halves (optional)

● In a small mixing bowl stir together snipped apricots, bran cereal, and orange juice. Let mixture stand about 5 minutes or till orange juice is absorbed.

● In a bowl beat margarine or butter with an electric mixer on medium to high speed about 30 seconds or till softened.

● Add about *half* of the flour, the sugar, brown sugar, egg, baking powder, vanilla, and cinnamon to the margarine. Beat till thoroughly combined, scraping sides of bowl occasionally. Then beat or stir in remaining flour and cereal mixture. Stir in chopped pecans.

● Drop dough from a rounded teaspoon 2 inches apart on a greased cookie sheet. If desired, lightly press a pecan half in center of each cookie. Bake in a 375° oven for 8 to 10 minutes or till edges are golden. Remove cookies and cool on a wire rack. Makes about 48.

Nutrition information per cookie: 63 calories, 1 g protein, 10 g carbohydrate, 3 g fat, 6 mg cholesterol, 38 mg sodium, 58 mg potassium.

# Currant Granola Mini-Bites

*Just the right size for the little ones. (Pictured at left.)*

¾ cup currants *or* 1 cup
    raisins *or* mixed dried
    fruit bits
½ cup margarine *or* butter
1 6-ounce can frozen apple
    juice concentrate
2 cups granola, slightly
    crushed
1¼ cups all-purpose flour
1 teaspoon baking soda
½ teaspoon finely shredded
    orange peel
½ teaspoon ground cinnamon

● In a medium saucepan heat currants, raisins, or fruit bits and margarine or butter till margarine is melted. Stir in apple juice concentrate and granola. Remove from heat.

● Add the flour, baking soda, orange peel, and cinnamon to mixture in saucepan. Stir till combined. Drop dough from a rounded teaspoon 2 inches apart on an ungreased cookie sheet. Bake in a 350° oven for 8 to 10 minutes or till edges are firm and bottoms are lightly browned. Remove cookies and cool on a wire rack. Makes about 40.

Nutrition information per cookie: 72 calories, 1 g protein, 9 g carbohydrate, 4 g fat, 0 mg cholesterol, 57 mg sodium, 65 mg potassium.

# Pineapple-Sour Cream Cookies

*For a truly pineapple-flavored cookie, frost these cakelike cookies with the Peaches 'n' Cream Frosting on page 18. Just substitute pineapple juice for the peach liquid in the frosting.*

½ cup margarine *or* butter
2½ cups all-purpose flour
1 8-ounce can crushed
     pineapple (juice pack),
     well drained
¾ cup packed brown sugar
½ cup sugar
½ cup dairy sour cream
     *or* plain yogurt
1 egg
½ teaspoon baking soda

● In a bowl beat margarine or butter with an electric mixer on medium to high speed about 30 seconds or till softened.

● Add about *half* of the flour, the pineapple, brown sugar, sugar, sour cream or yogurt, egg, and baking soda to the margarine. Beat till thoroughly combined, scraping sides of bowl occasionally. Then beat or stir in the remaining flour.

● Drop dough from a rounded teaspoon 2 inches apart on a greased cookie sheet. Bake in a 375° oven for 8 to 10 minutes or till edges are golden. Remove cookies and cool on a wire rack. Makes about 54.

Nutrition information per cookie: 64 calories, 1 g protein, 10 g carbohydrate, 2 g fat, 6 mg cholesterol, 34 mg sodium, 26 mg potassium.

# Walnut Wafers

*Team these crispy little wafers with ice cream for one great dessert.*

1 egg
½ cup packed brown sugar
2 tablespoons all-purpose
     flour
⅛ teaspoon salt
⅛ teaspoon baking powder
1¼ cups ground walnuts,
     toasted almonds,
     *or* pecans

● In a mixing bowl beat egg with an electric mixer on high speed about 2 minutes or till lemon colored.

● Add brown sugar to the egg. Beat about 2 minutes or till very thick. Then add flour, salt, and baking powder. Beat just till combined. Stir in the ground nuts.

● Drop nut mixture from a *level* teaspoon 2 inches apart on a greased, *foil-lined* cookie sheet. Bake in a 325° oven about 10 minutes or till edges are firm. Cool on the *foil-lined* cookie sheet for 2 minutes. Then remove the cookies and cool on a wire rack. Makes about 48.

Nutrition information per cookie: 31 calories, 1 g protein, 3 g carbohydrate, 2 g fat, 6 mg cholesterol, 9 mg sodium, 25 mg potassium.

# Saucepan Oatmeal Cookies

1 cup margarine *or* butter
1 cup sugar
1 cup packed brown sugar
2½ cups quick-cooking
    rolled oats
1¼ cups all-purpose flour
1 teaspoon baking powder
1 teaspoon baking soda
¼ teaspoon salt
2 well-beaten eggs
¼ cup chopped coconut
    (optional)
    Melted Chocolate (optional)

● In a medium saucepan combine margarine or butter, sugar, and brown sugar. Cook and stir over medium heat till melted. Remove from heat. Add oats, flour, baking powder, baking soda, and salt. Stir till combined. Add eggs, then mix well. If desired, stir in coconut.

● Drop batter from a rounded teaspoon 3 inches apart on a greased cookie sheet, stirring batter often. Bake in a 375° oven for 6 to 7 minutes or till edges are firm. Cool on cookie sheet for 1 minute. Remove cookies and cool on a wire rack. If desired, drizzle melted chocolate over cookies. Makes about 54.

**Melted Chocolate:** In a small heavy saucepan heat ½ cup *semisweet chocolate pieces* and 1 tablespoon *shortening* over low heat just till melted, stirring occasionally. Makes ⅓ cup.

Nutrition information per cookie: 87 calories, 1 g protein, 12 g carbohydrate, 4 g fat, 10 mg cholesterol, 79 mg sodium, 34 mg potassium.

# Florentines

*Crispy, candylike cookies topped with a thin layer of chocolate.*

⅓ cup margarine *or* butter
⅓ cup milk
¼ cup sugar
1 cup chopped almonds,
    toasted
¾ cup diced mixed candied
    fruits and peels, finely
    chopped
1 teaspoon finely shredded
    orange peel
¼ cup all-purpose flour
¾ cup semisweet chocolate
    pieces
2 tablespoons margarine
    *or* butter

● In a medium heavy saucepan combine ⅓ cup margarine or butter, milk, and sugar. Bring to a full rolling boil, stirring occasionally. Remove from heat. Stir in almonds, candied fruits and peels, and orange peel. Then stir in flour.

● Drop batter from a *level tablespoon* at least 3 inches apart on a *greased and floured* cookie sheet. (Grease and flour cookie sheet for each batch.) Then, using the back of a spoon, spread the batter into 3-inch circles. Bake in a 350° oven for 8 to 10 minutes or till edges are lightly browned. Cool on cookie sheet for 1 minute. Remove cookies and cool on waxed paper.

● In a small heavy saucepan heat chocolate pieces and 2 tablespoons margarine over low heat just till melted, stirring occasionally. Spread a *scant teaspoon* of the chocolate mixture evenly over the bottom of *each* cookie. When chocolate is *almost* set, use the tines of a fork to draw wavy lines through the chocolate. Store, covered, in the refrigerator. Makes about 24.

Nutrition information per cookie: 121 calories, 2 g protein, 12 g carbohydrate, 8 g fat, 0 mg cholesterol, 59 mg sodium, 72 mg potassium.

# Bar Cookies

*Whether gooey or cakelike, bar cookies are impossible to resist.*

## Basic Cake Brownies

*Here you'll find seven brownie recipes in one. For plain brownies, bake the Basic Cake Brownies; for fancier ones, try any of the six variations on pages 26–28.*

¾ cup sugar
⅓ cup margarine *or* butter
¼ cup unsweetened cocoa
    powder
1 egg
½ teaspoon vanilla
¾ cup all-purpose flour
¼ cup milk
¼ teaspoon baking powder
¼ teaspoon baking soda
½ cup chopped walnuts
    *or* pecans
1 tablespoon sugar (optional)
2 tablespoons chopped
    walnuts *or* pecans
    (optional)

● In a medium saucepan combine the ¾ cup sugar, margarine or butter, and cocoa powder. Cook and stir till margarine is melted. Remove from heat.

● Add egg and vanilla to saucepan. Using a wooden spoon, lightly beat just till combined. Add flour, milk, baking powder, and baking soda. Beat till well combined. Stir in ½ cup nuts.

● Spread batter into a greased 9x9x2-inch baking pan. If desired, for sugar-and-nut topping, sprinkle batter with 1 tablespoon sugar, then 2 tablespoons nuts. Bake in a 350° oven for 20 to 25 minutes or till a toothpick inserted near the center comes out clean. Cool in pan on a wire rack. Cut into bars. Makes 16 or 24.

Nutrition information per bar: 126 calories, 2 g protein, 7 g fat, 5 g carbohydrate, 17 mg cholesterol, 83 mg sodium, 47 mg potassium.

Candy-Topped
Brownies

Tri-Level
Brownies

German-Cake
Brownies

Cheesecake
Brownies

Nutty Caramel-
Topped Brownies

Basic Cake
Brownies

Tangerine-Macaroon
Brownies

# Cheesecake Brownies

*Psst . . . . The secret to perfect-looking dessert brownies is to line your baking pan with foil. This makes the brownies easy to remove. (Pictured on pages 24–25.)*

1 **recipe Basic Cake Brownies (see page 24)**
4 **3-ounce packages cream cheese, softened**
½ **cup sugar**
2 **eggs**
2 **tablespoons lemon juice Chocolate curls (optional)**

● For bottom layer, prepare batter for Basic Cake Brownies as directed. Spread batter into a greased, *foil-lined* 13x9x2-inch baking pan. Do not use sugar-nut topping. Bake in a 350° oven for 10 minutes.

● Meanwhile, for cheese layer, in a medium mixing bowl beat cream cheese and sugar with an electric mixer on medium to high speed till combined. Add eggs and lemon juice. Then beat just till combined.

● *Carefully* spread cheese mixture on top of partially baked brownies. Bake in the 350° oven for 15 to 20 minutes more or till center appears set and a knife inserted near center of cheese layer comes out clean. Cool in pan on a wire rack. Using the foil, lift brownies out of pan. Cut into bars. If desired, garnish with chocolate curls. Store, covered, in the refrigerator. Makes 24.

Nutrition information per bar: 156 calories, 3 g protein, 15 g carbohydrate, 10 g fat, 50 mg cholesterol, 103 mg sodium, 54 mg potassium.

# Nutty Caramel-Topped Brownies

*Just like a sundae, except that we put the caramel-nut topping over a brownie instead of ice cream. (Pictured on pages 24–25.)*

1 **recipe Basic Cake Brownies (see page 24)**
16 **vanilla caramels**
2 **tablespoons milk**
½ **cup semisweet chocolate pieces**
2 **tablespoons chopped pecans *or* walnuts**

● Prepare and bake Basic Cake Brownies as directed, *except* do not use the sugar-nut topping.

● Meanwhile, in a small heavy saucepan heat caramels and milk over low heat just till melted, stirring constantly.

● Sprinkle chocolate pieces on top of warm brownies. Then drizzle with the caramel mixture. Using a knife, *carefully* swirl the chocolate and caramel over the top of brownies to cover evenly. Sprinkle with nuts. If necessary, slightly pat nuts into caramel mixture. Cool in pan on a wire rack. Using a wet knife, cut into bars. Makes 16 or 24.

Nutrition information per bar: 194 calories, 3 g protein, 26 g carbohydrate, 10 g fat, 18 mg cholesterol, 105 mg sodium, 85 mg potassium.

# Tri-Level Brownies

*Rich chocolate brownies sandwiched between a crunchy oatmeal base and a smooth fudge frosting. (Pictured on pages 24–25.)*

1½ cups quick-cooking
    rolled oats
¾ cup all-purpose flour
1 cup packed brown sugar
¼ teaspoon baking soda
½ cup margarine *or* butter,
    melted
1 recipe Basic Cake Brownies
    (see page 24)
    Fudge Frosting
    Walnut halves (optional)

● For bottom layer, in a mixing bowl combine oats, flour, brown sugar, and baking soda. Stir in melted margarine or butter till well combined. Pat mixture into an ungreased 13x9x2-inch baking pan. Bake in a 350° oven for 5 minutes.

● Meanwhile, for middle layer, prepare batter for Basic Cake Brownies as directed. Spread brownie batter on top of baked bottom layer. Do not use sugar-nut topping.

● Bake in the 350° oven for 18 to 20 minutes more or till a toothpick inserted near center comes out clean. Cool in pan on a wire rack. Frost with Fudge Frosting. Cut into bars. If desired, garnish each bar with a walnut half. Makes 24 or 36.

**Fudge Frosting:** In a small saucepan heat 1 square (1 ounce) *unsweetened chocolate* and 2 tablespoons *margarine* or *butter* over low heat just till melted, stirring occasionally. Remove from heat. Stir in 1⅔ cups sifted *powdered sugar* and 1 teaspoon *vanilla.* Then stir in 1 to 2 tablespoons *hot water* to make frosting of soft-spreading consistency. Makes ¾ cup.

Nutrition information per frosted bar: 227 calories, 3 g protein, 33 g carbohydrate, 10 g fat, 12 mg cholesterol, 126 mg sodium, 95 mg potassium.

# Candy-Topped Brownies

*You might feel like a kid in a candy store when you try to decide which of the five candy toppers to use. (Pictured on pages 24–25.)*

1 recipe Basic Cake Brownies
    (see page 24)
½ cup candy-coated milk
    chocolate pieces;
    24 bite-size chocolate-
    covered peanut butter
    cups, 24 milk chocolate
    kisses, 24 milk chocolate
    stars, *or* 12 layered
    chocolate-mint wafers

● Prepare batter for Basic Cake Brownies as directed. Spread batter into the greased pan. Do not use sugar-nut topping.

● Bake in a 350° oven for 8 minutes. If using chocolate-mint wafers, cut them in half crosswise. Arrange candies on top of partially baked brownies (candies will sink slightly). Then bake in the 350° oven for 12 to 17 minutes more or till a toothpick inserted near the center comes out clean. Cool in pan on a wire rack. Cut into bars. Makes 16 or 24.

Nutrition information per bar: 157 calories, 2 g protein, 20 g carbohydrate, 8 g fat, 17 mg cholesterol, 83 mg sodium, 46 mg potassium.

# Tangerine-Macaroon Brownies

*Two treats in one! Citrus-flavored, coconut cookies on top of rich, cakey brownies. (Pictured on pages 24–25.)*

1 recipe Basic Cake Brownies
   (see page 24)
1 egg white
   Dash cream of tartar
¼ cup sugar
⅔ cup flaked coconut
1 teaspoon finely shredded
   tangerine peel *or*
   orange peel

● Prepare batter for Basic Brownies as directed. Spread batter into the greased pan. Do not use sugar-nut topping. Bake in a 350° oven for 10 minutes.

● Meanwhile, for topping, in a small mixing bowl beat egg white and cream of tartar with a rotary beater or an electric mixer on medium speed till soft peaks form (tips curl). Then gradually add sugar, beating till stiff peaks form (tips stand straight). Fold in coconut and peel.

● Spoon coconut mixture into *16* mounds on top of partially baked brownies. Then bake in the 350° oven for 10 to 15 minutes more or till coconut mixture is lightly browned and a toothpick inserted near center of brownie portion comes out clean. Cool in pan on a wire rack. Cut into bars by cutting between coconut mounds. Makes 16.

Nutrition information per bar: 154 calories, 2 g protein, 20 g carbohydrate, 8 g fat, 17 mg cholesterol, 87 mg sodium, 60 mg potassium.

# German-Cake Brownies

*German chocolate cake transformed into a brownie! (Pictured on pages 24–25.)*

1 recipe Basic Cake Brownies
   (see page 24)
1 egg yolk
¼ cup sugar
¼ cup milk
1 tablespoon margarine
   *or* butter
1 cup flaked coconut
⅓ cup chopped pecans

● Prepare and bake Basic Brownies as directed, *except* do not use the sugar-nut topping. Then cool in pan on a wire rack.

● Meanwhile, for topping, in a small saucepan use a fork to slightly beat egg yolk. Then stir in sugar, milk, and margarine or butter. Cook and stir over medium heat about 5 minutes or just till bubbly. Stir in coconut and pecans.

● Spread coconut mixture on top of brownies. Then broil 4 inches from the heat for 3 to 4 minutes or till slightly golden. Cool topping. Cut into bars. Makes 24.

Nutrition information per bar: 126 calories, 2 g protein, 14 g carbohydrate, 8 g fat, 23 mg cholesterol, 63 mg sodium, 52 mg potassium.

# Chocoladamias

*Chocolate lovers, here's a new heavenly treat—white chocolate-macadamia nut brownies.*

¼ cup margarine *or* butter
6 ounces white baking bar
    with cocoa butter
    *or* 1 cup white baking
    pieces with cocoa butter
2 eggs
¾ cup sugar
1¼ cups all-purpose flour
1 teaspoon vanilla
½ teaspoon baking powder
⅔ cup chopped macadamia
    nuts *or* toasted chopped
    almonds *or* pecans

● In a small heavy saucepan heat margarine or butter and *half* of white baking bar or pieces over low heat just till melted, stirring occasionally. (Mixture will separate.) Meanwhile, coarsely chop remaining white baking bar or pieces; set aside.

● In a mixing bowl beat eggs with an electric mixer till foamy. Add sugar, then beat on high speed for 1 minute till light. Add margarine mixture, flour, vanilla, and baking powder. Beat till thoroughly combined, scraping sides of bowl occasionally. Stir in nuts and remaining chopped white baking bar or pieces. Spread batter into a greased 9x9x2-inch baking pan. Bake in a 350° oven for 20 to 25 minutes or till top is golden and a toothpick inserted near center comes out clean. Cool in pan on a wire rack. Cut into bars. Makes 24.

Nutrition information per bar: 135 calories, 2 g protein, 16 g carbohydrate, 7 g fat, 24 mg cholesterol, 41 mg sodium, 48 mg potassium.

# Fruit Crumb Bars

*We've nicknamed these "Pick-a-Fruit Bars" because you can choose your favorite fruit filling. (Pictured on page 30.)*

2½ cups all-purpose flour
2½ cups quick-cooking
    rolled oats
1½ cups packed brown sugar
¼ teaspoon baking soda
1½ cups margarine *or* butter,
    melted
1 21- to 24-ounce can
    apple, apricot, blueberry,
    cherry, peach, *or* raisin
    pie filling; *or* 2 cups
    prepared mincemeat
1 teaspoon finely shredded
    lemon *or* orange peel
    Powdered Sugar Icing
    (optional)

In a mixing bowl stir together flour, oats, brown sugar, and baking soda. Then stir in melted margarine or butter till well combined. Set *2 cups* of the oat mixture aside for topper. Pat the remaining oat mixture into an ungreased 15x10x1-inch baking pan. Bake in a 350° oven for 12 minutes.

● If necessary, snip large pieces of fruit in pie filling. Stir lemon or orange peel into pie filling or mincemeat. *Carefully* spread on top of baked crust. Sprinkle with remaining oat mixture. Slightly pat oat mixture into filling. Bake in the 350° oven for 20 to 25 minutes more or till top is golden. Cool in pan on a wire rack. If desired, drizzle icing over bars. Cut into bars. Makes 50.

**Powdered Sugar Icing:** In a mixing bowl stir together 1 cup sifted *powdered sugar,* ¼ teaspoon *vanilla* or several drops *almond extract,* and 1 to 2 tablespoons *milk* to make of desired consistency. Makes about ⅓ cup.

Nutrition information per unglazed bar: 132 calories, 1 g protein, 19 g carbohydrate, 6 g fat, 0 mg cholesterol, 75 mg sodium, 46 mg potassium.

**Carrot-Orange-Yogurt Bars**

**Fruit Crumb Bars**
(see recipe, page 29)

**Pecan Pie Bars**

# Pecan Pie Bars

*For Chocolate Pecan Pie Bars: Stir ¼ cup miniature semisweet chocolate pieces into the egg mixture with the pecans.*

1¼ cups all-purpose flour
3 tablespoons brown sugar
½ cup margarine *or* butter
2 eggs
½ cup packed brown sugar
½ cup chopped pecans
½ cup light corn syrup
2 tablespoons margarine *or* butter, melted
1 teaspoon vanilla

● For crust, in a bowl stir together flour and 3 tablespoons brown sugar. Cut in ½ cup margarine or butter till mixture resembles coarse crumbs. Pat mixture into an ungreased 11x7x1½-inch baking pan. Bake in a 375° oven for 20 minutes.

● Meanwhile, for pecan layer, in another mixing bowl use a fork to beat eggs. Stir in ½ cup brown sugar, pecans, corn syrup, melted margarine or butter, and vanilla.

● Pour pecan mixture on top of crust, spreading evenly. Bake in the 375° oven for 15 to 20 minutes more or till center appears set. Slightly cool in pan on a wire rack, then cut into bars. Cool completely. Store bars, covered, in the refrigerator. Makes 24.

Nutrition information per bar: 132 calories, 1 g protein, 17 g carbohydrate, 7 g fat, 23 mg cholesterol, 68 mg sodium, 46 mg potassium.

# Carrot-Orange-Yogurt Bars

⅓ cup margarine *or* butter
1¼ cups all-purpose flour
1 cup sugar
½ cup orange *or* plain yogurt
1 egg
1 teaspoon baking powder
½ teaspoon finely shredded orange peel
¼ teaspoon baking soda
¾ cup finely shredded carrot (about 2 medium)
Orange Yogurt Frosting

● In a bowl beat margarine or butter with an electric mixer on medium to high speed about 30 seconds or till softened.

● Add about *half* of the flour, the sugar, yogurt, egg, baking powder, orange peel, and baking soda to the margarine. Beat till thoroughly combined, scraping sides of bowl occasionally. Then beat or stir in remaining flour. Stir in carrot.

● Spread batter into a greased 9x9x2-inch baking pan. Bake in a 350° oven for 25 to 30 minutes or till a toothpick inserted near center comes out clean. Cool in pan on a wire rack. Frost with Orange Yogurt Frosting. Cut into bars. Store, covered, in the refrigerator. Makes 24.

**Orange Yogurt Frosting:** In a small mixing bowl beat 2 tablespoons *orange* or *plain yogurt,* 1 tablespoon softened *margarine* or *butter,* and 1 teaspoon finely shredded *orange peel.* Gradually beat in 1½ to 1⅔ cups sifted *powdered sugar* to make frosting of spreading consistency. Makes about ⅔ cup.

Nutrition information per frosted bar: 118 calories, 1 g protein, 21 g carbohydrate, 3 g fat, 12 mg cholesterol, 90 mg sodium, 35 mg potassium.

# Full-of-Fruit Bars

*A fruit-lover's delight—cookies chock-full of pineapple and cherries.*

1 8-ounce can crushed
   pineapple (juice pack)
½ cup margarine *or* butter
1½ cups all-purpose flour
⅔ cup sugar
1 egg
½ teaspoon baking powder
½ teaspoon baking soda
½ cup finely chopped walnuts
½ cup maraschino cherries,
   coarsely chopped
   Pineapple Frosting
3 tablespoons chopped
   walnuts (optional)

● Drain pineapple well, reserving pineapple juice; set aside. In a mixing bowl beat margarine or butter with an electric mixer on medium to high speed about 30 seconds or till softened.

● Add pineapple, *¼ cup* reserved juice, about *half* of the flour, the sugar, egg, baking powder, and baking soda to the margarine. Beat till thoroughly combined, scraping sides of bowl occasionally. Then beat or stir in the remaining flour. Stir in ½ cup chopped walnuts and cherries.

● Spread batter into a greased 13x9x2-inch baking pan. Bake in a 350° oven for 20 to 25 minutes or till a toothpick inserted near center comes out clean. Cool in pan on a wire rack. Frost with Pineapple Frosting. If desired, sprinkle with 3 tablespoons chopped walnuts. Cut into bars. Makes 24.

**Pineapple Frosting:** In a medium mixing bowl beat 2½ cups sifted *powdered sugar,* 2 tablespoons *margarine* or *butter,* and *2 to 3 tablespoons* reserved *pineapple juice* or *milk* to make frosting of spreading consistency. Makes 1 cup.

Nutrition information per frosted bar: 163 calories, 2 g protein, 25 g carbohydrate, 7 g fat, 11 mg cholesterol, 89 mg sodium, 39 mg potassium.

# Whole Wheat Gingerbread Bars

½ cup shortening
1 cup all-purpose flour
½ cup whole wheat flour
½ cup light molasses
½ cup hot water
¼ cup packed brown sugar
1 egg
¾ teaspoon ground cinnamon
¾ teaspoon baking powder
½ teaspoon ground ginger
¼ teaspoon baking soda
¼ teaspoon salt
½ cup chopped walnuts
½ of a recipe Cream Cheese
   Frosting (see page 10)
   *or* powdered sugar

● In a mixing bowl beat shortening with an electric mixer on medium to high speed about 30 seconds or till softened. Add all-purpose flour, whole wheat flour, molasses, hot water, brown sugar, egg, cinnamon, baking powder, ginger, baking soda, and salt. Beat till thoroughly combined, scraping sides of bowl occasionally. Stir in walnuts.

● Spread batter into a greased 13x9x2-inch baking pan. Bake in a 375° oven about 25 minutes or till a toothpick inserted near center comes out clean. Cool in pan on a wire rack. Frost with Cream Cheese Frosting or sift powdered sugar over top. Cut into bars. Store frosted bars, covered, in the refrigerator. Makes 36.

Nutrition information per frosted bar: 93 calories, 1 g protein, 11 g carbohydrate, 5 g fat, 9 mg cholesterol, 44 mg sodium, 76 mg potassium.

# Pumpkin Bars

*Presto! Substitute 16 ounces applesauce for the pumpkin and you'll have Applesauce Bars.*

2 cups all-purpose flour
1½ cups sugar
2 teaspoons baking powder
2 teaspoons ground cinnamon
1 teaspoon baking soda
¼ teaspoon salt
¼ teaspoon ground cloves
1 16-ounce can pumpkin
1 cup cooking oil
4 beaten eggs
1 cup chopped walnuts (optional)
Cream Cheese Frosting (see recipe, page 10) *or* powdered sugar

● In a mixing bowl stir together flour, sugar, baking powder, cinnamon, baking soda, salt, and cloves. Stir in pumpkin, cooking oil, and eggs till thoroughly combined. Then, if desired, stir in walnuts.

● Spread batter into an ungreased 15x10x1-inch baking pan. Bake in a 350° oven for 25 to 30 minutes or till a toothpick inserted near center comes out clean. Cool in pan on a wire rack. Frost with Cream Cheese Frosting or sift powdered sugar over top. Cut into bars. Store frosted bars, covered, in the refrigerator. Makes 48.

Nutrition information per frosted bar: 124 calories, 1 g protein, 15 g carbohydrate, 7 g fat, 25 mg cholesterol, 69 mg sodium, 34 mg potassium.

# Peanut Butter and Chocolate Chip Bars

*For an oatmeal version, reduce the flour to 1 cup and stir in ¾ cup of quick-cooking rolled oats with the peanuts.*

¾ cup peanut butter
¼ cup cooking oil
1½ cups all-purpose flour
1 cup packed brown sugar
2 eggs
¾ cup milk
½ teaspoon baking powder
¼ teaspoon baking soda
½ cup miniature semisweet chocolate pieces
⅓ cup chopped peanuts

● In a bowl beat peanut butter and oil with an electric mixer on low to medium speed about 30 seconds or till combined.

● Add about *half* of the flour, the brown sugar, eggs, *half* of the milk, baking powder, and baking soda to the peanut butter mixture. Beat till thoroughly combined, scraping sides of bowl occasionally. Then beat or stir in the remaining flour and remaining milk. Stir in chocolate pieces and chopped peanuts.

● Spread batter into a greased 13x9x2-inch baking pan. Bake in a 350° oven for 25 to 30 minutes or till a toothpick inserted near center comes out clean. Cool in pan on a wire rack. Frost with Peanut Butter Frosting. Cut into bars. Makes 36.

**Peanut Butter Frosting:** In a mixing bowl beat 3½ cups sifted *powdered sugar*, ¼ cup *peanut butter*, and ¼ to ⅓ cup *milk* to make frosting of spreading consistency. Makes 1½ cups.

Nutrition information per frosted bar: 163 calories, 4 g protein, 23 g carbohydrate, 7 g fat, 16 mg cholesterol, 61 mg sodium, 107 mg potassium.

Mixed-Nut
Squares

Chocolate Revel Bars

Chewy Peanut Candy-Layer Bars
(see recipe, page 36)

# Mixed-Nut Squares

*A nut-lover's delight!*

¼ cup margarine *or* butter
1 cup all-purpose flour
1 cup packed brown sugar
1 egg
1 teaspoon baking powder
½ teaspoon vanilla
1 cup mixed nuts, Brazil
    nuts, *or* cashews,
    coarsely chopped

● In a medium saucepan heat margarine or butter till melted. Remove from heat.

● Add flour, brown sugar, egg, baking powder, and vanilla to the margarine in saucepan. Using a wooden spoon, beat just till combined. Stir in nuts.

● Spread batter into a greased 8x8x2-inch baking pan. Bake in a 350° oven for 20 to 25 minutes or till a toothpick inserted near center comes out clean. Slightly cool in pan on a wire rack. Cut into bars, then cool completely in pan. Makes 16.

Nutrition information per bar: 162 calories, 3 g protein, 22 g carbohydrate, 7 g fat, 17 mg cholesterol, 119 mg sodium, 111 mg potassium.

# Chocolate Revel Bars

*For Whole Wheat Chocolate Revel Bars: Prepare the Chocolate Revel Bars as directed below, except substitute 1 cup whole wheat flour for 1 cup of all-purpose flour.*

1 cup margarine *or* butter
2½ cups all-purpose flour
2 cups packed brown sugar
2 eggs
4 teaspoons vanilla
1 teaspoon baking soda
3 cups quick-cooking
    rolled oats
1 14-ounce can (1¼ cups)
    *sweetened condensed*
    milk
1½ cups semisweet chocolate
    pieces
2 tablespoons margarine
    *or* butter
½ cup chopped walnuts
    *or* pecans

● In a mixing bowl beat 1 cup margarine or butter with an electric mixer on medium to high speed about 30 seconds or till softened. Add about *half* of the flour, the brown sugar, eggs, *2 teaspoons* of the vanilla, and baking soda. Beat till thoroughly combined, scraping sides of bowl occasionally. Then beat or stir in remaining flour. Stir in oats. Set oat mixture aside.

● In a medium saucepan heat sweetened condensed milk, chocolate pieces, and 2 tablespoons margarine or butter over low heat just till chocolate is melted, stirring occasionally. Remove from heat. Stir in walnuts and the remaining 2 teaspoons vanilla.

● For crust, pat *two-thirds* (about 3⅓ cups) of the oat mixture into an ungreased 15x10x1-inch baking pan. Then spread chocolate mixture on top of crust. Drop the remaining oat mixture by teaspoonfuls on top of chocolate layer. Bake in a 350° oven about 25 minutes or till top is lightly golden (chocolate layer will still look slightly moist). Cool in pan on a wire rack. Cut into bars. Makes 60.

Nutrition information per bar: 145 calories, 2 g protein, 20 g carbohydrate, 7 g fat, 12 mg cholesterol, 72 mg sodium, 93 mg potassium.

# Apple Pie Bars

2 to 3 medium cooking apples, peeled, cored, and coarsely chopped (2 cups)
⅓ cup apple juice *or* water
½ teaspoon ground cinnamon
⅛ teaspoon ground nutmeg
¼ cup sugar
2 teaspoons cornstarch
½ cup margarine *or* butter
1½ cups all-purpose flour
½ cup sugar
1 egg
½ teaspoon baking powder

● For filling, in medium saucepan combine apples, apple juice or water, cinnamon, and nutmeg. Cook over medium heat till boiling, stirring occasionally. Stir together ¼ cup sugar and cornstarch. Then stir sugar mixture into boiling mixture. Cook and stir till thickened and bubbly. Remove from heat. Set filling aside to slightly cool.

● Meanwhile, for crust, in a mixing bowl beat margarine or butter with an electric mixer on medium to high speed about 30 seconds or till softened. Add about *half* of the flour, the ½ cup sugar, egg, and baking powder. Beat till thoroughly combined, scraping sides of bowl occasionally. Then beat or stir in remaining flour. Pat *two-thirds* (about 1 cup) into an ungreased 9x9x2-inch baking pan. Spread filling on top of crust. Drop the remaining dough by small teaspoonfuls on top of apple filling. Bake in a 375° oven about 30 minutes or till top is golden. Cool in pan on a wire rack. Cut into bars. Makes 24.

Nutrition information per bar: 98 calories, 1 g protein, 14 g carbohydrate, 4 g fat, 11 mg cholesterol, 54 mg sodium, 29 mg potassium.

# Chewy Peanut Candy-Layer Bars

*Reminiscent of a peanut-nougat candy bar. (Pictured on page 34.)*

½ cup margarine *or* butter
½ cup packed brown sugar
¼ teaspoon salt
1 cup all-purpose flour
1½ cups tiny marshmallows
⅓ cup sugar
⅓ cup light corn syrup
⅓ cup peanut butter
1 cup crisp rice cereal
1 cup unsalted dry roasted peanuts

● For crust, in a mixing bowl beat margarine or butter with an electric mixer on medium to high speed about 30 seconds or till softened. Add brown sugar and salt. Beat till thoroughly combined, scraping bowl occasionally. Stir in flour. Pat mixture into an ungreased 11x7x1½-inch baking pan. Bake in a 350° oven for 12 to 15 minutes or till lightly brown. Sprinkle marshmallows on top of baked crust. Then bake in the 350° oven for 1 to 3 minutes more or till marshmallows are puffy. Set aside on a wire rack.

● For top layer, in a medium saucepan combine sugar and corn syrup. Cook and stir till sugar is dissolved. Then stir in peanut butter till melted. Remove from heat and stir in cereal and peanuts. Spoon cereal mixture on top of marshmallow layer. Then *carefully* spread cereal mixture over marshmallow layer. Cool in pan on a wire rack. Cut into bars. Makes 35.

Nutrition information per bar: 112 calories, 2 g protein, 13 g carbohydrate, 6 g fat, 0 mg cholesterol, 71 mg sodium, 63 mg potassium.

# Oatmeal-Caramel Bars

*Mmmm—a rich and gooey candylike cookie.*

1½ cups quick-cooking
   rolled oats
¾ cup all-purpose flour
⅔ cup packed brown sugar
¼ teaspoon baking soda
⅔ cup margarine *or* butter,
   melted
25 vanilla caramels
2 tablespoons margarine
   *or* butter
1 tablespoon milk
½ cup chopped nuts
⅓ cup miniature semisweet
   chocolate pieces

● In a bowl stir together oats, flour, brown sugar, and baking soda. Then stir in the melted margarine or butter till well combined. Set *1 cup* of the oat mixture aside for topper.

● Pat the remaining oat mixture into a *foil-lined* 8x8x2-inch baking pan. Bake in a 350° oven for 10 minutes.

● Meanwhile, for filling, in a small heavy saucepan combine caramels, 2 tablespoons margarine or butter, and milk. Cook and stir over low heat just till melted.

● *Carefully* spread filling on top of baked crust. Sprinkle with nuts, chocolate pieces, and remaining oat mixture. Bake in the 350° oven about 20 minutes more or till top is golden. Cool in pan on a wire rack. Using the foil, lift out of the pan. Cut into bars. Makes 24

Nutrition information per bar: 177 calories, 2 g protein, 22 g carbohydrate, 10 g fat, 0 mg cholesterol, 107 mg sodium, 85 mg potassium.

# Backpackers Snackbars

*Need a quick energy boost? Then grab one of these.*

⅓ cup margarine *or* butter
½ cup packed brown sugar
½ cup quick-cooking
   rolled oats
⅓ cup all-purpose flour
⅓ cup whole wheat flour
2 tablespoons toasted
   wheat germ
2 beaten eggs
¼ cup packed brown sugar
½ cup sliced almonds
½ cup flaked coconut
¼ cup raisins

● For crust, in a bowl beat margarine or butter with an electric mixer on medium to high speed about 30 seconds or till softened. Add ½ cup brown sugar. Beat till fluffy, scraping sides of bowl occasionally. Stir in oats, all-purpose flour, whole wheat flour, and wheat germ. Pat mixture into an ungreased 9x9x2-inch baking pan. Bake in a 350° oven for 10 minutes.

● Meanwhile, in a small mixing bowl stir together eggs and ¼ cup brown sugar till well combined. Then stir in almonds, coconut, and raisins.

● Pour nut mixture on top of crust, spreading evenly. Bake in a 350° oven about 20 minutes or till center appears set. Cool slightly in pan on a wire rack, then score into bars. Cool completely. Cut into bars. Makes 24.

Nutrition information per bar: 98 calories, 13 g protein, 5 g carbohydrate, 5 g fat, 23 mg cholesterol, 39 mg sodium, 77 mg potassium.

## Sliced Cookies

*Have freshly baked cookies at a moment's notice when you keep cookie-dough rolls on hand in your refrigerator or freezer.*

## Basic Sliced Cookies

*Here you'll find seven sliced-cookie recipes in one. For plain cookies, bake the Basic Sliced Cookies; for fancier ones, try any of the variations on pages 40–42.*

½ cup shortening
½ cup margarine *or* butter
3 cups all-purpose flour
1 cup sugar
1 egg
2 tablespoons milk
1 teaspoon vanilla
½ teaspoon baking soda
¼ teaspoon salt

● In a mixing bowl beat shortening and margarine or butter with an electric mixer on medium to high speed about 30 seconds or till softened.

● Add about *half* of the flour, the sugar, egg, milk, vanilla, baking soda, and salt to the shortening mixture. Beat till thoroughly combined, scraping sides of bowl occasionally. Then beat or stir in the remaining flour.

● Shape dough into *two* 8-inch rolls. Wrap in waxed paper or clear plastic wrap. Chill for 4 to 24 hours.

● Cut dough into ¼-inch-thick slices. Place 2 inches apart on an ungreased cookie sheet. Bake in a 375° oven for 8 to 10 minutes or till edges are firm and bottoms are lightly browned. Remove cookies and cool on a wire rack. Makes about 60.

Nutrition information per cookie: 60 calories, 1 g protein, 3 g fat, 8 g carbohydrate, 5 mg cholesterol, 38 mg sodium, 9 mg potassium.

Spumoni Slices

Basic Sliced Cookies

Chocolate
Grasshopper
Cookies

Peppermint Pinwheels

Double Almond Cookies

Chocolate Star Tassies

Mocha Slices

# Chocolate Grasshopper Cookies

*If you don't have any crème de menthe, substitute ¼ cup milk, ¼ teaspoon peppermint extract, and a few drops of green food coloring. (Pictured on pages 38–39.)*

1 **recipe Basic Sliced Cookies (see page 38)**
½ **cup unsweetened cocoa powder**
¼ **cup margarine *or* butter**
2½ **to 3 cups sifted powdered sugar**
¼ **cup crème de menthe**

● Prepare dough for Basic Sliced Cookies as directed, *except* reduce flour to *2½ cups* and mix in cocoa powder with the sugar. Shape and chill as directed.

● Cut dough into ⅛-inch-thick slices. Place 2 inches apart on an ungreased cookie sheet. Bake in a 375° oven for 7 to 9 minutes or till tops look dry. Remove cookies; cool on wire rack.

● For filling, in a large mixing bowl beat margarine or butter with an electric mixer on medium to high speed about 30 seconds or till softened. Gradually beat in *2 cups* of the powdered sugar. Beat in crème de menthe till smooth. Then gradually beat in enough of the remaining powdered sugar to make frosting of spreading consistency.

● To assemble, frost bottoms of *half* of the cookies with 1 to 2 teaspoons filling. Then top *each* with the remaining unfrosted cookies, bottom side down. Makes about 60.

Nutrition information per cookie: 90 calories, 1 g protein, 13 g carbohydrate, 4 g fat, 5 mg cholesterol, 52 mg sodium, 13 mg potassium.

# Double Almond Cookies

*Full of lots of almond goodness! (Pictured on pages 38–39.)*

1 **recipe Basic Sliced Cookies (see page 38)**
1 **8-ounce can almond paste**
⅓ **cup sugar**
¼ **cup milk**
⅔ **cup sliced almonds**

● Prepare and chill dough for Basic Sliced Cookies as directed.

● For topping, crumble almond paste into a mixing bowl. Add sugar and milk, then beat with an electric mixer till smooth.

● Cut dough into ¼-inch-thick slices. Place 2 inches apart on an ungreased cookie sheet. Spread about *1 teaspoon* of almond topping on top of *each* cookie. Sprinkle with several sliced almonds. Bake and cool as directed. Makes about 60.

Nutrition information per cookie: 93 calories, 1 g protein, 11 g carbohydrate, 5 g fat, 5 mg cholesterol, 39 mg sodium, 42 mg potassium.

# Peppermint Pinwheels

*For Citrus Pinwheels: Substitute 2 teaspoons finely shredded orange peel for the peppermint extract, and tint the dough using ¼ teaspoon red food coloring plus ¼ teaspoon yellow food coloring. (Peppermint Pinwheels are pictured on pages 38–39.)*

1 **recipe Basic Sliced Cookies (see page 38)**
¾ teaspoon peppermint extract
½ teaspoon red food coloring

● Prepare dough for Basic Sliced Cookies as directed. Divide dough in half. Set *1 portion* aside. To the remaining portion knead in peppermint extract and food coloring.

● To shape dough, between 2 sheets of waxed paper roll *each* portion into a 12x11-inch rectangle. Remove top sheets of waxed paper from plain and pink doughs. Invert plain dough on top of pink dough. Peel off top sheet of paper. From the long side, roll up jelly-roll style, removing bottom sheet of paper as you roll. Cut roll crosswise in half, then wrap and chill for 4 to 24 hours. Slice, bake, and cool as directed. Makes about 48.

Nutrition information per cookie: 82 calories, 1 g protein, 10 g carbohydrate, 4 g fat, 6 mg cholesterol, 47 mg sodium, 11 mg potassium.

# Mocha Slices

*So easy, yet so elegant. (Pictured on pages 38–39.)*

1 **tablespoon instant coffee crystals**
1 teaspoon water
1 **recipe Basic Sliced Cookies (see page 38)**
½ cup unsweetened cocoa powder
¾ teaspoon ground cinnamon
1 12-ounce package (2 cups) milk chocolate pieces
¼ cup shortening
1 6-ounce package (1 cup) semisweet chocolate pieces (optional)
2 tablespoons shortening (optional)

● In a custard cup stir together coffee crystals and water till dissolved. Prepare dough for Basic Sliced Cookies as directed, *except* reduce flour to *2½ cups.* Mix in cocoa powder, cinnamon, and coffee with the sugar. Shape and chill as directed.

● Cut dough into ⅛-inch-thick slices. Place 2 inches apart on an ungreased cookie sheet. Bake in a 375° oven for 7 to 9 minutes or till tops look dry. Remove cookies. Cool on wire rack.

● In a heavy saucepan heat milk chocolate pieces and ¼ cup shortening over low heat just till melted, stirring occasionally. Dip half of *each* cookie into milk chocolate mixture. Place on waxed paper and let stand till chocolate is set.

● If desired, in another heavy saucepan heat the semisweet chocolate pieces and 2 tablespoons shortening over low heat just till melted, stirring occasionally. Dip part of *each* cookie again into semisweet chocolate mixture. Place again on waxed paper and let stand till chocolate is set. Makes about 108.

Nutrition information per cookie: 56 calories, 1 g protein, 6 g carbohydrate, 4 g fat, 4 mg cholesterol, 27 mg sodium, 20 mg potassium.

# Spumoni Slices

*Take one bite, and you'll discover a cookie with the same luscious flavors as spumoni, an Italian ice cream. (Pictured on pages 38–39.)*

1 **recipe Basic Sliced Cookies (see page 38)**
1 **square (1 ounce) semisweet chocolate, melted and cooled**
4 **teaspoons milk**
⅓ **cup chopped candied red cherries**
   **Few drops red food coloring**
½ **cup finely chopped pistachio nuts**
¼ **teaspoon rum flavoring**
   **Few drops green food coloring**

● Prepare dough for Basic Sliced Cookies as directed. Divide dough into thirds.

● To *1 portion,* mix in chocolate and *2 teaspoons* of the milk; set aside. To *another portion,* mix in cherries and enough red food coloring to tint dough pink; set aside. To *remaining portion,* mix in nuts, remaining 2 teaspoons milk, rum flavoring, and enough green food coloring to tint dough green.

● To shape dough, line bottom and sides of an 8x4x2-inch loaf pan with waxed paper or clear plastic wrap. Press pink dough evenly in pan. Top with chocolate dough. Then top with green dough. Cover and chill for 4 to 24 hours.

● Invert pan to remove dough. Remove waxed paper or plastic wrap. Cut dough into ¼-inch-thick slices, then cut *each* slice crosswise into *3* pieces. Place 2 inches apart on an ungreased cookie sheet. Bake and cool as directed. Makes about 84.

Nutrition information per cookie: 55 calories, 1 g protein, 7 g carbohydrate, 3 g fat, 3 mg cholesterol, 27 mg sodium, 17 mg potassium.

# Chocolate Star Tassies

*Our easy recipe forms tassie cups in seconds. (Pictured on pages 38–39.)*

1 **recipe Basic Sliced Cookies (see page 38)**
½ **cup unsweetened cocoa powder**
80 **milk chocolate stars or bite-size chocolate-covered peanut butter cups**

● Prepare dough for Basic Sliced Cookies as directed, *except* reduce flour to 2½ cups and mix in cocoa powder with the sugar. Shape and chill as directed.

● Cut dough into ¾-inch-thick slices. Then cut *each* slice into quarters. Place each quarter into an ungreased 1¾-inch muffin cup. (Or, shape each quarter into a ball, place on an ungreased cookie sheet, then make an indentation in center of each.) Bake in a 375° oven for 8 to 10 minutes or till tops look dry. *Immediately* press a chocolate star or peanut butter cup gently and evenly into *each* cookie. Cool cookies in muffin pan for 1 minute. Then remove and cool on a wire rack. Makes about 80.

Nutrition information per cookie: 69 calories, 1 g protein, 8 g carbohydrate, 4 g fat, 4 mg cholesterol, 36 mg sodium, 25 mg potassium.

# Spicy Oatmeal Refrigerated Cookies

½ cup shortening
½ cup margarine *or* butter
1¾ cups all-purpose flour
1 cup packed brown sugar
1 egg
1 teaspoon ground cinnamon
½ teaspoon baking soda
½ teaspoon vanilla
⅛ teaspoon ground cloves
1 cup quick-cooking
    rolled oats
½ cup finely chopped walnuts

● In a bowl beat shortening and margarine with an electric mixer on medium to high speed 30 seconds or till softened.

● Add about *half* of the flour, the brown sugar, egg, cinnamon, baking soda, vanilla, and cloves to the shortening mixture. Beat till thoroughly combined, scraping sides of bowl occasionally. Then beat or stir in remaining flour. Stir in oats and walnuts. Shape dough into *two* 8-inch rolls. Wrap in waxed paper or clear plastic wrap, then chill for 4 to 24 hours.

● Cut dough into ¼-inch-thick slices. Place 1 inch apart on an ungreased cookie sheet. Bake in a 375° oven for 7 to 9 minutes or till edges are lightly browned. Cool on cookie sheet 1 minute. Then remove cookies and cool on a wire rack. Makes about 60.

Nutrition information per cookie: 68 calories, 1 g protein, 7 g carbohydrate, 4 g fat, 5 mg cholesterol, 30 mg sodium, 28 mg potassium.

# Date Pinwheel Cookies

1 8-ounce package (1⅓ cups)
    pitted whole dates,
    snipped
⅓ cup sugar
½ cup water
2 tablespoons lemon juice
1½ teaspoons vanilla
½ cup shortening
½ cup margarine *or* butter
3 cups all-purpose flour
½ cup sugar
½ cup packed brown sugar
1 egg
3 tablespoons milk
½ teaspoon baking soda
¼ teaspoon salt

● For filling, in a medium saucepan combine snipped dates, ⅓ cup sugar, and water. Bring to boiling, then reduce heat. Cook and stir about 2 minutes or till thickened. Stir in lemon juice and ½ *teaspoon* of the vanilla. Set filling aside to cool.

● In a bowl beat shortening and margarine or butter with an electric mixer on medium to high speed about 30 seconds or till softened. Add *half* of the flour, the ½ cup sugar, brown sugar, egg, milk, baking soda, salt, and remaining 1 teaspoon vanilla. Beat till thoroughly combined. Beat or stir in remaining flour. Cover and chill for 1 hour or till easy to handle.

● Divide dough in half. To shape dough, between 2 sheets of waxed paper roll *each* portion into a 12x10-inch rectangle. Remove top sheets of waxed paper. Spread with filling. From long side, roll up *each*, jelly-roll style, removing bottom sheet of paper as you roll. Moisten and pinch edges to seal. Wrap in waxed paper or clear plastic wrap. Chill for 4 to 24 hours.

● Cut into ¼-inch slices. Place 2 inches apart on a greased cookie sheet. Bake in a 375° oven 10 to 12 minutes or till lightly browned. Remove cookies. Cool on a wire rack. Makes about 80.

Nutrition information per cookie: 61 calories, 1 g protein, 10 g carbohydrate, 3 g fat, 3 mg cholesterol, 28 mg sodium, 30 mg potassium.

**Brown Sugar Slices**

Red Raspberry
Twirls
(see recipe, page 46)

# Brown Sugar Slices

*The added hint of spice makes these cookies satisfying with or without the frosting. (Pictured at left and on the cover.)*

½ cup shortening
½ cup margarine *or* butter
3 cups all-purpose flour
1 cup packed brown sugar
1 egg
2 tablespoons milk
1 teaspoon vanilla
½ teaspoon baking soda
½ teaspoon ground ginger
¼ teaspoon salt
⅛ teaspoon ground nutmeg
   Brown Sugar Frosting

● In a mixing bowl beat shortening and margarine or butter with an electric mixer on medium to high speed about 30 seconds or till softened.

● Add about *half* of the flour, the brown sugar, egg, milk, vanilla, baking soda, ginger, salt, and nutmeg to shortening mixture. Beat till thoroughly combined. Then beat or stir in the remaining flour. Shape dough into *two* 8-inch rolls. Wrap in waxed paper or clear plastic wrap, then chill for 4 to 24 hours.

● Cut dough into ¼-inch-thick slices. Place 2 inches apart on an ungreased cookie sheet. Bake in a 375° oven for 8 to 10 minutes or till edges are firm. Remove cookies. Cool on a wire rack. Drizzle with Brown Sugar Frosting. Makes about 60.

**Brown Sugar Frosting:** In a small saucepan melt 3 tablespoons *margarine* or *butter.* Stir in ⅓ cup packed *brown sugar.* Then cook and stir till bubbly. Remove from heat. Stir in ⅔ cup sifted *powdered sugar* and 1 to 2 tablespoons *milk* to make frosting of drizzling consistency. Makes ½ cup.

Nutrition information per frosted cookie: 81 calories, 1 g protein, 11 g carbohydrate, 4 g fat, 5 mg cholesterol, 46 mg sodium, 26 mg potassium.

# Orange Slices

½ cup shortening
½ cup margarine *or* butter
3 cups all-purpose flour
1 cup sugar
1 egg
2 tablespoons finely
   shredded orange peel
2 tablespoons orange juice
¼ teaspoon baking soda

● In a mixing bowl beat shortening and margarine or butter with an electric mixer on medium to high speed about 30 seconds or till softened.

● Add about *half* of the flour, the sugar, egg, orange peel, orange juice, and baking soda to shortening mixture. Beat till thoroughly combined. Beat or stir in the remaining flour. Shape dough into *two* 8-inch rolls. Wrap in waxed paper or clear plastic wrap, then chill for 4 to 24 hours.

● Cut dough into ¼-inch-thick slices. Place 2 inches apart on an ungreased cookie sheet. Bake in a 375° oven for 8 to 10 minutes or till bottoms are lightly browned. Remove cookies and cool on a wire rack. Makes about 60.

Nutrition information per cookie: 66 calories, 1 g protein, 8 g carbohydrate, 3 g fat, 5 mg cholesterol, 24 mg sodium, 9 mg potassium.

# Almond Bites

½ of an 8-ounce can (about ½ cup) almond paste
½ cup margarine *or* butter
1½ cups all-purpose flour
½ cup sugar
1 egg
½ teaspoon finely shredded orange peel
¼ teaspoon baking powder
Blanched whole almonds, toasted
1 slightly beaten egg white
2 teaspoons water

● Crumble almond paste into a mixing bowl. Add margarine or butter, then beat with an electric mixer on medium to high speed for 1 to 2 minutes or till combined.

● Add about *half* of the flour, the sugar, egg, orange peel, and baking powder to the almond mixture. Beat till thoroughly combined, scraping sides of bowl occasionally. Then beat or stir in remaining flour. Shape dough into *two* 7-inch rolls. Wrap in waxed paper or clear plastic wrap. Chill for 4 to 24 hours.

● Cut dough into ⅛-inch-thick slices. Place 1½ inches apart on an ungreased cookie sheet. Lightly press a whole almond in center of each. Mix egg white with water. Brush tops of cookies and almonds with mixture. Bake in a 350° oven for 7 to 9 minutes or till golden. Remove; cool on a rack. Makes about 96.

Nutrition information per cookie: 41 calories, 1 g protein, 4 g carbohydrate, 3 g fat, 3 mg cholesterol, 14 mg sodium, 29 mg potassium.

# Red Raspberry Twirls

*A pretty gift cookie for a special friend. (Pictured on page 44 and on the cover.)*

½ cup margarine *or* butter
2¾ cups all-purpose flour
1 cup sugar
1 egg
3 tablespoons milk
½ teaspoon baking powder
¼ teaspoon almond extract (optional)
½ cup seedless red raspberry jam
1½ teaspoons cornstarch
½ cup toasted almonds, ground

● In a mixing bowl beat margarine with an electric mixer on medium to high speed about 30 seconds or till softened. Add *1 cup* of the flour, the sugar, egg, milk, baking powder, and almond extract, if desired. Beat till combined. Then beat or stir in remaining flour. Cover and chill 1 hour or till easy to handle.

● For filling, in a saucepan combine jam and cornstarch. Cook and stir till thickened and bubbly. Cook and stir for 1 minute more. Stir in almonds. Cover and set aside to cool slightly.

● Divide dough in half. On waxed paper use a floured rolling pin to roll *each* portion into a 12x8-inch rectangle. Spread with filling. From short side, roll up *each,* jelly-roll style, removing waxed paper as you roll. Moisten; pinch edges to seal. Wrap in waxed paper or clear plastic wrap. Chill for 4 to 24 hours.

● Cut dough into ¼-inch-thick slices. Place 2 inches apart on a greased, *foil-lined* cookie sheet. Bake in a 375° oven for 9 to 11 minutes or till edges are firm and bottoms are lightly browned. Remove cookies and cool on a wire rack. Makes about 60.

Nutrition information per cookie: 60 calories, 1 g protein, 10 g carbohydrate, 2 g fat, 5 mg cholesterol, 22 mg sodium, 16 mg potassium.

# Plain 'n' Peanutty Rolls

*A ribbon of peanut butter winds its way through a rich buttery cookie.*

3½ cups all-purpose flour
1½ cups sifted powdered sugar
1½ cups margarine *or* butter
 ½ cup dairy sour cream
 ½ cup creamy peanut butter
 1 tablespoon milk
  Melted Chocolate (see
    recipe, page 23)

● In a mixing bowl stir together flour and powdered sugar. Cut in margarine or butter till mixture resembles coarse crumbs. Divide crumb mixture in half. To *1 portion* of crumb mixture, stir in sour cream till mixture forms a ball. To *remaining portion,* stir in peanut butter and milk till mixture forms a ball. Then divide *each* dough mixture in half.

● To shape dough, on a lightly powdered-sugared surface, roll *each* dough portion into a 12x9-inch rectangle. Place a peanut butter rectangle on top of *each* plain rectangle. From the long side, roll up *each* stack, jelly-roll style. Wrap in waxed paper or clear plastic wrap. Chill for 1 to 2 hours or till firm.

● Cut dough into ½-inch-thick slices. Place 2 inches apart on an ungreased cookie sheet. Bake in a 350° oven for 18 to 20 minutes or till edges are slightly brown. Remove cookies. Cool on a wire rack. Drizzle with Melted Chocolate. Makes about 48.

Nutrition information per cookie: 129 calories, 2 g protein, 12 g carbohydrate, 9 g fat, 1 mg cholesterol, 81 mg sodium, 40 mg potassium.

# Lemon Poppy Seed Slices

 ½ cup shortening
 ½ cup margarine *or* butter
2½ cups all-purpose flour
 1 cup sugar
 1 egg
 1 tablespoon milk
 ½ teaspoon baking powder
 2 tablespoons finely
    shredded lemon peel
    (use 2 to 3 lemons)
 2 tablespoons poppy seed

● In a mixing bowl beat shortening and margarine or butter with an electric mixer on medium to high speed about 30 seconds or till softened.

● Add about *half* of the flour, the sugar, egg, milk, and baking powder to the shortening mixture. Beat till thoroughly combined, scraping sides of bowl occasionally. Then beat or stir in remaining flour, lemon peel, and poppy seed.

● Shape dough into *two* 8-inch rolls. Wrap in waxed paper or clear plastic wrap, then chill for 4 to 24 hours.

● Cut dough into ¼-inch-thick slices. Place 2 inches apart on an ungreased cookie sheet. Bake in a 375° oven for 8 to 10 minutes or till edges are firm and bottoms are lightly browned. Remove cookies and cool on a wire rack. Makes about 60.

Nutrition information per cookie: 63 calories, 1 g protein, 7 g carbohydrate, 3 g fat, 5 mg cholesterol, 22 mg sodium, 10 mg potassium.

# Shaped Cookies

*Create a choice of cookie shapes by forming dough into various designs.*

## Basic Scottish Shortbread

*Here you'll find seven shaped-cookie recipes in one. For plain shortbread, bake the Basic Scottish Shortbread; for fancier cookies, try any of the six variations on pages 50–52.*

1¼  cups all-purpose flour
 3  tablespoons sugar
 ½  cup butter

● In a mixing bowl stir together the flour and sugar. Then cut in butter till mixture resembles fine crumbs. Form mixture into a ball and knead till smooth.

● For wedges, on an ungreased cookie sheet pat or roll dough into an 8-inch circle. Using your fingers, press to make a scalloped edge. If desired, use a fork to prick the dough. Using a sharp knife, cut dough circle into 12 to 16 pie-shaped wedges. Do not separate wedges.

● Bake in a 325° oven for 25 to 30 minutes or just till edges are lightly browned. Cut into wedges again. Then remove wedges and cool on a wire rack. Makes 12 to 16.

Nutrition information per cookie: 128 calories, 1 g protein, 8 g fat, 13 g carbohydrate, 21 mg cholesterol, 79 mg sodium, 15 mg potassium.

**Basic Scottish Shortbread**

**Spicy Shortbread Nuggets**

Crunchy
Almond
Sticks

Cherry
Shortbread
Cookies

Oatmeal
Shortbread

Coconut-Lemon
Squares

Preserves
'n' Shortbread
Cookies

# Preserves 'n' Shortbread Cookies

*To prevent the filled cookies from breaking, only slightly indent the shortbread before baking. (Pictured on pages 48–49.)*

1 **recipe Basic Scottish Shortbread (see page 48)**
¼ **cup seedless strawberry** *or* **blackberry preserves,** *or* **seedless red raspberry jam**
½ **of a recipe Powdered Sugar Icing (see page 29)**

● Prepare dough for Basic Scottish Shortbread as directed.

● After kneading dough, divide dough in half. Shape *each* portion into an 8-inch roll. Place the rolls 4 to 5 inches apart on an ungreased cookie sheet. Pat each roll into a 2-inch-wide strip. Using the back of a spoon, slightly press a 1-inch-wide indentation lengthwise down the center of each strip.

● Bake in a 325° oven for 20 to 25 minutes or till edges are lightly browned. Transfer cookie sheet to a wire rack. If necessary, re-form the indentations in the shortbread. Then *immediately* spoon the preserves or jam evenly into the indentations. While shortbread still is warm, diagonally cut the strips crosswise into 1-inch-wide pieces. Drizzle with Powdered Sugar Icing. Cool completely, then remove cookies from cookie sheet. Makes about 18.

Nutrition information per frosted cookie: 108 calories, 1 g protein, 15 g carbohydrate, 5 g fat, 14 mg cholesterol, 53 mg sodium, 15 mg potassium.

# Crunchy Almond Sticks

*So buttery and rich, they'll melt in your mouth. (Pictured on pages 48–49.)*

1 **recipe Basic Scottish Shortbread (see page 48)**
½ **teaspoon vanilla**
½ **teaspoon almond extract Milk**
¼ **cup sliced almonds, toasted**
½ **of a recipe Powdered Sugar Icing (see page 29)**

● Prepare dough for Basic Scottish Shortbread as directed, *except* before kneading, mix in vanilla and almond extract.

● After kneading dough, on an ungreased cookie sheet pat or roll dough into a 10x6-inch rectangle. Generously brush top with milk, then sprinkle with almonds. Bake as directed.

● While shortbread still is warm, cut rectangle into 3x1-inch sticks. Remove and cool on a wire rack. Drizzle with Powdered Sugar Icing. Makes 20.

Nutrition information per frosted cookie: 94 calories, 1 g protein, 11 g carbohydrate, 5 g fat, 13 mg cholesterol, 48 mg sodium, 19 mg potassium.

# Spicy Shortbread Nuggets

*Grab a handful—these flavor-packed nuggets are so tasty, you can't stop with just one. (Pictured on pages 48–49.)*

1 recipe Basic Scottish
  Shortbread (see page 48)
¼ cup packed brown sugar
½ teaspoon aniseed,
  crushed
¼ teaspoon ground cinnamon
⅛ teaspoon ground cloves
⅛ teaspoon ground
  cardamom

● Prepare dough for Basic Scottish Shortbread as directed, *except* substitute ¼ cup brown sugar for 3 tablespoons sugar. Mix in aniseed, cinnamon, cloves, and cardamom with the flour.

● For nuggets*, after kneading dough, divide dough into *12* portions. On a lightly floured surface roll *each* portion of dough into a 10-inch-long rope. Cut ropes into ½-inch-long pieces. Place pieces ½ inch apart in an ungreased shallow baking pan. Bake in a 325° oven for 12 to 15 minutes or till edges are firm and bottoms are lightly browned. Remove cookies and cool on paper towels. Makes about 20 dozen.

Nutrition information per 10 nugget-shaped cookies: 67 calories, 1 g protein, 7 g carbohydrate, 4 g fat, 10 mg cholesterol, 40 mg sodium, 16 mg potassium.

*For wafers, pat or roll dough into an 8-inch square. Using a fluted pastry wheel or knife, cut into 1-inch squares. Place 1 inch apart on an ungreased cookie sheet. Bake in a 325° oven about 20 minutes or till bottoms are lightly browned. Remove and cool on wire rack. Makes 64.

Nutrition information per wafer-shaped cookie: 25 calories, 0 g protein, 3 g carbohydrate, 1 g fat, 4 mg cholesterol, 15 mg sodium, 6 mg potassium.

# Oatmeal Shortbread

*Doll up shortbread with melted chocolate and chopped nuts. (Pictured on pages 48–49.)*

1 recipe Basic Scottish
  Shortbread (see page 48)
⅓ cup quick-cooking
  rolled oats

● Prepare dough for Basic Scottish Shortbread as directed, *except* reduce flour to *1 cup*. After cutting in butter, stir in oats.

● After kneading dough, on an ungreased cookie sheet pat or roll dough into a 10x6-inch rectangle. Bake as directed.

● While shortbread still is warm, cut rectangle into 3x1-inch sticks. Remove and cool on a wire rack. Makes 20.

Nutrition information per cookie: 76 calories, 1 g protein, 8 g carbohydrate, 5 g fat, 12 mg cholesterol, 47 mg sodium, 12 mg potassium.

# Cherry Shortbread Cookies

*Flecks of cherries and a hint of nutmeg turn shortbread into something simply sensational. (Pictured on pages 48–49.)*

½ cup maraschino cherries, well drained
1 recipe Basic Scottish Shortbread (see page 48)
¼ teaspoon ground nutmeg
2 to 3 drops red food coloring (optional)

● Place cherries on paper towels to absorb excess juice. Prepare dough for Basic Scottish Shortbread as directed, *except* mix in nutmeg with the flour. Before kneading, mix in cherries and food coloring, if desired.

● After kneading dough, shape dough into 1-inch balls. Place 2 inches apart on an ungreased cookie sheet. Using the bottom of a glass, slightly flatten balls to ½ inch. Bake in a 325° oven about 20 minutes or till edges are firm and bottoms are lightly browned. Remove cookies. Cool on a wire rack. Makes about 24.

Nutrition information per cookie: 68 calories, 1 g protein, 8 g carbohydrate, 4 g fat, 10 mg cholesterol, 39 mg sodium, 8 mg potassium.

# Coconut-Lemon Squares

*Transform shortbread into a delicious crust for the zesty lemon-and-coconut filling. (Pictured on pages 48–49.)*

1 recipe Basic Scottish Shortbread (see page 48)
2 eggs
¾ cup sugar
2 tablespoons all-purpose flour
1 teaspoon finely shredded lemon peel
3 tablespoons lemon juice
½ teaspoon baking powder
¼ teaspoon salt
1 cup coconut
Powdered sugar (optional)

● For crust, prepare dough for Basic Scottish Shortbread as directed. After kneading dough, pat dough into an ungreased 9x9x2-inch baking pan. Bake in a 350° oven for 15 minutes.

● Meanwhile, for lemon mixture, in a mixing bowl beat eggs with an electric mixer till foamy. Add sugar, flour, lemon juice, baking powder, and salt. Beat on medium speed about 3 minutes or till slightly thickened, scraping sides of bowl occasionally. Stir in lemon peel and coconut.

● Pour lemon mixture on top of crust. Bake in the 350° oven for 20 to 25 minutes more or till lightly golden around edges and center is set. Cool in pan on a wire rack. If desired, sift powdered sugar over top. Cut into bars. Makes 16 or 24.

Nutrition information per bar: 168 calories, 2 g protein, 22 g carbohydrate, 8 g fat, 50 mg cholesterol, 110 mg sodium, 40 mg potassium.

# Peanut Butter Crisscrosses

*For Peanut-Butter Kiss Cookies: Do not flatten before baking. Then, after baking, slightly press a milk chocolate kiss into each hot cookie.*

½ cup peanut butter
¼ cup shortening
¼ cup margarine *or* butter
1⅓ cups all-purpose flour
½ cup sugar
½ cup packed brown sugar
1 egg
1 teaspoon vanilla
½ teaspoon baking powder
½ teaspoon baking soda
   Sugar

● In a bowl beat peanut butter, shortening, and margarine or butter with an electric mixer on medium to high speed about 30 seconds or till softened.

● Add about *half* of the flour, the ½ cup sugar, brown sugar, egg, vanilla, baking powder, and baking soda to the peanut butter mixture. Beat till thoroughly combined, scraping sides of bowl occasionally. Then beat or stir in the remaining flour. If necessary, cover and chill dough till easy to handle.

● Shape dough into 1-inch balls. Place 2 inches apart on an ungreased cookie sheet. Using the tines of a fork dipped in additional sugar, flatten balls to about ¼ inch by pressing fork in 2 directions to form crisscross marks. Bake in a 350° oven for 10 to 12 minutes or till bottoms are lightly browned. Remove cookies and cool on a wire rack. Makes about 54.

Nutrition information per cookie: 61 calories, 1 g protein, 7 g carbohydrate, 3 g fat, 5 mg cholesterol, 36 mg sodium, 28 mg potassium.

# Snickerdoodles

*No time to shape the dough into balls? Then forget the chilling, drop the dough from a spoon onto a cookie sheet, and sprinkle with the sugar-cinnamon mixture.*

½ cup margarine *or* butter
1½ cups all-purpose flour
1 cup sugar
1 egg
½ teaspoon vanilla
¼ teaspoon baking soda
¼ teaspoon cream of tartar
2 tablespoons sugar
1 teaspoon ground cinnamon

● In a bowl beat margarine or butter with an electric mixer on medium to high speed about 30 seconds or till softened.

● Add about *half* of the flour, the 1 cup sugar, egg, vanilla, baking soda, and cream of tartar to the margarine. Beat till thoroughly combined, scraping sides of bowl occasionally. Then beat or stir in remaining flour. Cover and chill for 1 hour.

● In a shallow dish combine the 2 tablespoons sugar and cinnamon. Shape dough into 1-inch balls, then roll balls in the sugar-cinnamon mixture. Place 2 inches apart onto an ungreased cookie sheet. Bake in a 375° oven for 10 to 11 minutes or till edges are golden. Remove cookies and cool on a wire rack. Makes about 36.

Nutrition information per cookie: 68 calories, 1 g protein, 10 g carbohydrate, 3 g fat, 8 mg cholesterol, 40 mg sodium, 9 mg potassium.

Molded Cookies

# Gingersnaps

2¼ cups all-purpose flour
1 cup packed brown sugar
¾ cup shortening *or* cooking oil
¼ cup molasses
1 egg
1 teaspoon baking soda
1 teaspoon ground ginger
1 teaspoon ground cinnamon
½ teaspoon ground cloves
¼ cup sugar

● In a mixing bowl beat *half* of the flour, the brown sugar, shortening or cooking oil, molasses, egg, baking soda, ginger, cinnamon, and cloves with an electric mixer on medium to high speed till thoroughly combined. Beat or stir in remaining flour.

● Shape dough into 1-inch balls. Roll balls in sugar. Place 2 inches apart on an ungreased cookie sheet. Bake in a 375° oven for 8 to 10 minutes or till tops are crackled and cookies appear set. Remove cookies. Cool on a wire rack. Makes about 48.

Nutrition information per cookie: 76 calories, 1 g protein, 11 g carbohydrate, 3 g fat, 6 mg cholesterol, 27 mg sodium, 42 mg potassium.

# Molded Cookies

*For a splash of color, paint the baked cookies with food coloring diluted with water.*

¾ cup margarine *or* butter
3 cups all-purpose flour
1 cup sugar
1 egg yolk
¼ cup milk
1 teaspoon ground cinnamon
1 teaspoon ground cardamom
¼ teaspoon baking powder
¼ teaspoon ground cloves

● In a bowl beat margarine or butter with an electric mixer on medium to high speed about 30 seconds or till softened. Add *1 cup* of the flour, the sugar, egg yolk, milk, cinnamon, cardamom, baking powder, and cloves. Beat till thoroughly combined, scraping the sides of the bowl occasionally. Then stir in remaining flour.

● For large cookies*, lightly oil a ceramic or wooden cookie mold. Press dough firmly into the mold. Level dough in mold. Then unmold dough onto a greased cookie sheet. Repeat with remaining dough, placing cookies 2 inches apart on the cookie sheet. Bake in a 375° oven for 10 to 14 minutes or till edges are lightly browned. Cool on cookie sheet for 1 minute. Then remove cookies and cool on a wire rack. Makes 10 to 16.

Nutrition information per large cookie: 346 calories, 5 g protein, 49 g carbohydrate, 15 g fat, 28 mg cholesterol, 173 mg sodium, 58 mg potassium.

*For individual cookies, shape dough into 1- to 1¼-inch balls. Place 2 inches apart on a greased cookie sheet. Using a *floured* cookie stamp or a *floured* bottom of a glass, flatten balls to ⅛- to ¼-inch thickness. If desired, trim dough around edges of stamp or glass. Bake in the 375° oven for 8 to 10 minutes or till lightly browned. Remove; cool on a rack. Makes 30 to 48.

Nutrition information per individual cookie: 115 calories, 2 g protein, 16 g carbohydrate, 5 g fat, 9 mg cholesterol, 58 mg sodium, 19 mg potassium.

# Cutout Cookies

*For easier handling, roll out only half of the dough at a time, keeping the remaining dough chilled until you need it.*

## Basic Sugar Cutouts

*Here you'll find seven cutout-cookie recipes in one. For plain cookies, bake the Basic Sugar Cutouts; for fancier ones, try any of the six variations on pages 58–60.*

⅓ cup shortening
⅓ cup margarine *or* butter
2 cups all-purpose flour
¾ cup sugar
1 egg
1 tablespoon milk
1 teaspoon baking powder
1 teaspoon vanilla
Decorative candies *or* colored sugar (optional)
Creamy white frosting mix for a 1-layer cake, prepared (optional)

● In a mixing bowl beat shortening and margarine or butter with an electric mixer on medium to high speed about 30 seconds or till softened.

● Add about *half* of the flour, the sugar, egg, milk, baking powder, and vanilla to the shortening mixture. Beat till thoroughly combined, scraping sides of bowl occasionally. Beat or stir in remaining flour. Divide dough in half. Cover; chill for 1 to 2 hours or till easy to handle.

● On a lightly floured surface roll *each* portion of dough to ⅛-inch thickness. Cut into desired shapes. Place 1 inch apart on an ungreased cookie sheet. If desired, sprinkle with candies or colored sugar before baking.

● Bake in a 375° oven for 7 to 9 minutes or till edges are firm and bottoms are very lightly browned. Remove cookies and cool on a wire rack. If desired, decorate cookies with frosting, then sprinkle with decorative candies or colored sugar. Makes 36 to 48.

Nutrition information per cookie: 75 calories, 1 g protein, 4 g fat, 10 g carbohydrate, 8 mg cholesterol, 31 mg sodium, 10 mg potassium.

Basic Sugar
Cutouts

Rye Wafers

Chocolate Sugar Cutouts

Window Cutouts

Lemon Pillows

Caramel-Nut
Sandwiches

Aniseed Cookies

# Chocolate Sugar Cutouts

*Mix and match the cookie cutouts—bake a batch of chocolate and a batch of basic cutouts, then "glue" them together with a little frosting. (Pictured on pages 56–57.)*

1 recipe Basic Sugar Cutouts
  (see page 56)
⅓ cup unsweetened cocoa
  powder

● Prepare dough for Basic Sugar Cutouts as directed, *except* mix in the cocoa powder with the sugar. Divide the dough and chill it as directed.

● Then roll, cut out, bake, and decorate the cookies as directed. Makes 36 to 48.

Nutrition information per cookie: 78 calories, 1 g protein, 10 g carbohydrate, 4 g fat, 8 mg cholesterol, 36 mg sodium, 15 mg potassium.

# Aniseed Cookies

*Just a sprinkle adds the sparkle. Look for coarse-grain sanding sugar at a candy supply store, or use granulated sugar. (Pictured on pages 56–57.)*

1 recipe Basic Sugar Cutouts
  (see page 56)
2 teaspoons aniseed, crushed
1 beaten egg white
  Sanding sugar *or* sugar

● Prepare dough for Basic Sugar Cutouts as directed, *except* mix in the aniseed with the sugar. Then divide the dough and chill it as directed.

● After rolling out dough, cut dough into desired small shapes. Place 1 inch apart on an ungreased cookie sheet. Brush tops with egg white, then sprinkle with sanding sugar. Bake and cool as directed. Makes about 60.

Nutrition information per cookie: 47 calories, 1 g protein, 6 g carbohydrate, 2 g fat, 5 mg cholesterol, 19 mg sodium, 8 mg potassium.

# Window Cutouts

*For Chocolate Window Cutouts: Use the Chocolate Sugar Cutouts on opposite page. (Pictured on pages 56–57.)*

1 recipe Basic Sugar Cutouts
  (see page 56)
1½ cups sifted powdered sugar
¼ cup cherry, currant, *or* red
  raspberry jelly
  Powdered sugar (optional)
  Cherry, currant, *or* red
  raspberry jelly (optional)

● Prepare and chill dough for Basic Sugar Cutouts as directed.

● After rolling out dough, cut dough into 3-inch shapes. Then, using a 1- to 1½-inch cookie cutter, cut holes in the centers of *half* of the cookies. Bake and cool as directed.

● Meanwhile, for filling, in a mixing bowl stir together 1½ cups powdered sugar and ¼ cup jelly till well combined.

● To assemble, if desired, sift additional powdered sugar over tops of cookies *with* holes in centers. Spread filling on the bottoms of the cookies *without* holes. Then top *each* of these cookies with the remaining cookies, powdered sugar side up. If desired, fill the hole of each cookie with a small spoonful of additional jelly. Makes about 24.

Nutrition information per cookie: 146 calories, 1 g protein, 23 g carbohydrate, 6 g fat, 11 mg cholesterol, 46 mg sodium, 18 mg potassium.

# Rye Wafers

*The rye flour turns the basic sugar cookie into a slightly nutty-flavored wafer. (Pictured on pages 56–57.)*

1 recipe Basic Sugar Cutouts
  (see page 56)
1 cup rye flour
  Melted Chocolate
  (see recipe, page 23)
  (optional)

● Prepare dough for Basic Sugar Cutouts as directed, *except* substitute 1 cup rye flour for 1 cup of the all-purpose flour. Divide dough and chill it as directed.

● After rolling out dough, cut dough into small circle, square, or triangle shapes. Bake and cool as directed. If desired, drizzle with Melted Chocolate. Makes about 60.

Nutrition information per cookie: 43 calories, 1 g protein, 5 g carbohydrate, 2 g fat, 5 mg cholesterol, 18 mg sodium, 7 mg potassium.

# Caramel-Nut Sandwiches

*For other delicious fillings, sandwich fruit-flavored, soft-style cream cheese, peanut butter, or jam between the crisp cookies. (Pictured on pages 56–57.)*

| | |
|---|---|
| 1 recipe Basic Sugar Cutouts (see page 56) | ● Prepare and chill dough for Basic Sugar Cutouts as directed. |

2 tablespoons finely chopped pecans
32 vanilla *or* chocolate caramels
2 tablespoons milk

● On a lightly floured surface roll *each* portion of dough into a 12x11-inch rectangle. Using a fluted pastry wheel, cut dough into 2x1-inch rectangles. Place 1 inch apart on an ungreased cookie sheet. Sprinkle *half* of the cookies with the finely chopped pecans. Slightly pat nuts into the cookies. Bake and cool as directed.

● For filling, in a small heavy saucepan heat caramels and milk over low heat just till melted, stirring constantly. Cool slightly.

● To assemble, spread filling on the bottoms of the cookies *without* nuts. Then top *each* of these cookies with remaining cookies, nut side up. Makes about 60.

Nutrition information per cookie: 67 calories, 1 g protein, 10 g carbohydrate, 3 g fat, 5 mg cholesterol, 30 mg sodium, 17 mg potassium.

# Lemon Pillows

*Chocolate nestled inside a citrus-flavored cookie. (Pictured on pages 56–57.)*

1 recipe Basic Sugar Cutouts (see page 56)
1 tablespoon finely shredded lemon *or* orange peel
2 4-ounce bars milk chocolate
Powdered sugar

● Prepare dough for Basic Sugar Cookie Cutouts as directed, *except* reduce margarine to ¼ *cup.* Mix in lemon or orange peel with the sugar. Do *not* divide dough in half. Cover and chill for 1 to 2 hours or till easy to handle. Meanwhile, break or cut *each* chocolate bar into *fourteen* 1½x1-inch rectangles.

● On a lightly floured surface roll *all* of the dough into a 17½x12-inch rectangle. Cut dough into *twenty-eight* 3x2½-inch rectangles.

● To assemble, place a piece of chocolate near the short side of *each* dough rectangle. Fold the other side of dough rectangle over chocolate. Using the tines of a fork, seal edges. Bake and cool as directed. Sift powdered sugar over tops. Makes 28.

Nutrition information per cookie: 138 calories, 2 g protein, 18 g carbohydrate, 7 g fat, 11 mg cholesterol, 41 mg sodium, 44 mg potassium.

**Whole Wheat Critters**
(see recipe, page 62)

Whole Wheat Crit...

1 cup Margarine or ...
3 cups Whole Wheat S...
1¼ cups Packed brow...
2 eggs
2 teaspoons baking ...
1 teaspoon Vanilla...
2 tablespoon...
½ teaspoon...

# Gingerbread People

*Giant gingerbread cookies like grandma used to make. If you prefer thinner, 2½- to 3-inch cookies, then bake the cookies for 5 to 6 minutes.*

| | |
|---|---|
| ½ | cup shortening |
| 2½ | cups all-purpose flour |
| ½ | cup sugar |
| ½ | cup molasses |
| 1 | egg |
| 1 | tablespoon vinegar |
| 1 | teaspoon baking powder |
| 1 | teaspoon ground ginger |
| ½ | teaspoon baking soda |
| ½ | teaspoon ground cinnamon |
| ½ | teaspoon ground cloves |
| | Powdered Sugar Icing (see recipe, page 29) |
| | Decorative candies (optional) |

● In a mixing bowl beat shortening with an electric mixer on medium to high speed about 30 seconds or till softened. Add about *half* of the flour, the sugar, molasses, egg, vinegar, baking powder, ginger, baking soda, cinnamon, and cloves. Beat till thoroughly combined, scraping sides of bowl occasionally. Then beat or stir in the remaining flour. Divide dough in half. Cover and chill about 3 hours or till easy to handle.

● On a lightly floured surface roll *each* portion of dough to ¼-inch thickness. Cut into 4½- to 6-inch-long people shapes. Place 1 inch apart on a greased cookie sheet.

● Bake in a 375° oven for 6 to 8 minutes or till edges are firm and bottoms are very lightly browned. Cool on cookie sheet for 1 minute. Remove cookies and cool on a wire rack. Decorate cookies with icing. Then sprinkle with decorative candies, if desired. Makes 12 to 18.

Nutrition information per frosted cookie: 273 calories, 3 g protein, 45 g carbohydrate, 10 g fat, 23 mg cholesterol, 84 mg sodium, 182 mg potassium.

# Whole Wheat Critters

*A slightly sweet, crackerlike cookie. (Pictured on page 61.)*

| | |
|---|---|
| 1 | cup margarine *or* butter |
| 3 | cups whole wheat flour |
| 1¼ | cups packed brown sugar |
| 2 | eggs |
| 2 | teaspoons baking powder |
| 1 | teaspoon vanilla |
| 2 | tablespoons sugar |
| ½ | teaspoon ground nutmeg |

● In a mixing bowl beat margarine with an electric mixer on medium to high speed about 30 seconds or till softened. Add about *half* of the whole wheat flour, the brown sugar, eggs, baking powder, and vanilla. Beat till thoroughly combined, scraping sides of bowl occasionally. Then beat or stir in the remaining flour. Divide dough in half. Cover and chill about 3 hours or till easy to handle.

● On a lightly floured surface roll *each* portion of dough to ⅛-inch thickness. Cut into desired animal shapes. Place 1 inch apart on an ungreased cookie sheet. If desired, use a fork to prick the cookies. Stir together sugar and nutmeg, then sprinkle on tops of cookies. Bake in a 350° oven for 8 to 10 minutes or till edges are firm and bottoms are very lightly browned. Remove cookies. Cool on a wire rack. Makes about 40.

Nutrition information per cookie: 103 calories, 2 g protein, 14 g carbohydrate, 5 g fat, 14 mg cholesterol, 74 mg sodium, 63 mg potassium.

# No-Fuss Festive Cookies

Long for homemade cookies during the holidays, but don't have the time to bake? In this chapter, you'll find a treasury of super-speedy, festive-looking cookies that'll fit into even the busiest schedule.

## Baking Pleasures

### Kid Helpers

Kids and cookies: you can't ask for a better combination. Not only do kids love to eat cookies, but they also like to make them.

When young cooks want to help, let them mix and shape the dough with their hands, roll it out and cut it out with cookie cutters, drop the dough from a spoon, spread it into a pan, or decorate cookies with colored sugars, candies, and frostings or icings.

For the more difficult steps, such as beating with an electric mixer, transferring cookie sheets to or from the hot oven, and chopping nuts, you'll need to judge how much supervision your children will need.

### Hosting a Holiday Cookie Exchange

Christmastime means cookie time—trays filled with lots of different kinds of festive cookies. But with the hustle and bustle of shopping, parties, and working, often it's difficult to find the time to bake a variety of holiday cookies.

Well, here's an easy solution: Gather four to ten of your friends together for a cookie exchange.

Ask each person to bring one-half dozen of cookies for *each* participant, including himself or herself, plus a few extra cookies for a "tasting plate."

Also, have everyone bring an empty container for taking cookies home. (All containers and lids should be marked with the owner's name to prevent mix-ups.)

If you and your friends like to share recipes, ask them to bring copies of their cookie recipes too.

Have a long table or counter ready where containers can be placed as guests arrive. Have your guests help divide cookies among the containers, as well as the "tasting plate." Then set out the plate of cookies for all to enjoy.

# Amaretti Cookies

*On holidays, give a gift of Italian almond macaroons. Wrap individual cookies in square pieces of brightly colored tissue paper and place in a decorative tin.*

2 egg whites
2 teaspoons amaretto
   liqueur *or* ½ teaspoon
   almond extract
½ teaspoon vanilla
¼ teaspoon cream of tartar
½ cup sugar
1½ cups ground almonds

● Line a cookie sheet with brown paper, parchment paper, or foil. Set cookie sheet aside.

● In a medium mixing bowl beat egg whites, amaretto liqueur or almond extract, vanilla, and cream of tartar with an electric mixer on medium speed till soft peaks form (tips curl). Gradually add sugar, beating till stiff peaks form (tips stand straight). Fold in ground almonds.

● Drop almond mixture from a rounded teaspoon 1½ inches apart on the prepared cookie sheet. Bake in a 300° oven for 15 to 18 minutes or just till beginning to brown. Turn oven off and leave door closed. Let cookies dry in the oven for 30 minutes. Then remove the cookies and cool them completely on a wire rack. Makes about 24.

Nutrition information per cookie: 61 calories, 2 g protein, 6 g carbohydrate, 4 g fat, 0 mg cholesterol, 5 mg sodium, 57 mg potassium.

# Trick-or-Treat Cookies

*As a trick, leave the candy out of some of the cookies.*

¾ cup margarine *or* butter
2 cups all-purpose flour
½ cup sugar
1 egg
1 teaspoon vanilla
   Small gumdrops, chocolate-
   covered milk caramel
   balls, *or* candy-coated
   peanuts
   Orange Glaze
   Chocolate-flavored
   sprinkles

● In a bowl beat margarine or butter with an electric mixer on medium to high speed about 30 seconds or till softened. Add about *half* of flour, the sugar, egg, and vanilla. Beat till thoroughly combined. Then beat or stir in the remaining flour.

● For each cookie, shape a *level tablespoon* of dough around a piece of candy to form a ball. Place 1 inch apart on an ungreased cookie sheet. Bake in a 350° oven about 15 minutes or till edges are firm and bottoms are lightly browned. Remove cookies and cool on a wire rack. Dip tops of cookies in Orange Glaze, then sprinkle with chocolate sprinkles. If desired, serve cookies in small decorative paper cups. Makes about 30.

**Orange Glaze:** In a mixing bowl stir together 1 cup sifted *powdered sugar*, ¼ teaspoon *vanilla*, 4 drops *yellow food coloring*, 1 drop *red food coloring*, and 4 to 5 teaspoons *milk* to make of dipping consistency. Makes ⅓ cup.

Nutrition information per glazed cookie: 107 calories, 1 g protein, 15 g carbohydrate, 5 g fat, 9 mg cholesterol, 59 mg sodium, 14 mg potassium.

# Basic Holiday Cookies

*Here you'll find seven holiday-cookie recipes in one. For plain cookies, bake the Basic Holiday Cookies; for fancier ones, try any of the six variations on pages 68–70.*

¾  cup margarine *or* butter
1¾  cups all-purpose
    flour
½  cup sugar
1  egg yolk
½  teaspoon vanilla
¼  teaspoon baking powder
¼  teaspoon almond extract
    *or* coconut flavoring
    (optional)
    Desired food coloring
    (optional)
    Desired decorative candies
    *or* colored sugars

● In a bowl beat margarine with an electric mixer on medium to high speed about 30 seconds or till softened.
● Add about *half* of the flour, the sugar, egg yolk, vanilla, baking powder, and almond extract or coconut flavoring (if desired) to the margarine. Beat till thoroughly combined. Then beat or stir in the remaining flour. If desired, tint dough with food coloring (or divide dough into thirds; tint each portion a different color). *Do not chill dough.*
● Pack dough into a cookie press. Force dough through a cookie press onto an ungreased cookie sheet. (Or, drop dough from a rounded teaspoon 1 inch apart on the cookie sheet; flatten slightly.) If desired, decorate cookies with candies or colored sugars. Bake in a 375° oven for 8 to 10 minutes or till edges are firm but not browned. Remove cookies and cool on a wire rack. Makes about 42.

Nutrition information per cookie: 59 calories, 1 g protein, 3 g fat, 6 g carbohydrate, 6 mg cholesterol, 40 mg sodium, 7 mg potassium.

**Sugar Bells**

**Easy Candy Canes**

Holiday
Checkerboards

Florentine Triangles

Snowcapped Balls

Basic
Holiday Cookies

Cherry Nests

# Snowcapped Balls

*A must for your holiday cookie tray. Serve these delicious little snow-covered cookies in decorative paper cups for a special touch. (Pictured on pages 66–67.)*

| |
|---|
| 1 **recipe Basic Holiday Cookies (see page 66)** |
| ½ **cup miniature semisweet chocolate pieces** *or* **very finely chopped walnuts, pecans,** *or* **almonds** |
| 1 **cup sifted powdered sugar** |

● Prepare dough for Basic Holiday Cookies as directed, *except* do not tint dough. Stir or knead in chocolate pieces or nuts.

● Shape dough into 1-inch balls. Place 1 inch apart on an ungreased cookie sheet. Bake in a 325° oven for 15 to 17 minutes or till the edges are firm and the bottoms are very lightly browned.

● Remove cookies and cool *slightly* on a wire rack. In a paper or plastic bag gently shake a few warm cookies at a time in the powdered sugar. Then cool completely on the wire rack. If necessary, sift additional powdered sugar over tops of the cooled cookies. Makes about 42.

Nutrition information per cookie: 78 calories, 1 g protein, 10 g carbohydrate, 4 g fat, 6 mg cholesterol, 40 mg sodium, 14 mg potassium.

# Cherry Nests

*Unexpected guests dropping by during the holidays? No problem when you keep a batch of these cherry-nut balls on hand in the freezer. (Pictured on pages 66–67.)*

| |
|---|
| 1 **recipe Basic Holiday Cookies (see page 66)** |
| 1 **egg white** |
| 1½ **cups very finely chopped hazelnuts (filberts), pecans,** *or* **walnuts** |
| **Candied cherries, halved** |

● Prepare dough for Basic Holiday Cookies as directed.

● In a shallow dish, use a fork to slightly beat egg white with 1 tablespoon *water.* Shape dough into 1-inch balls. Dip balls into egg white mixture, then roll in chopped nuts. Place 2 inches apart on an ungreased cookie sheet. Press a cherry half in center of each cookie. Bake in a 325° oven for 15 to 17 minutes or till edges are firm and bottoms are very lightly browned. Remove cookies and cool on a wire rack. Makes about 42.

Nutrition information per cookie: 91 calories, 1 g protein, 9 g carbohydrate, 6 g fat, 6 mg cholesterol, 42 mg sodium, 30 mg potassium.

# Easy Candy Canes

*Adding the finishing touch is simple when you use purchased tubes of decorator icing. (Pictured on pages 66–67.)*

1 recipe Basic Holiday
    Cookies (see page 66)
¼ teaspoon peppermint
    extract *or* 2 drops oil
    of cinnamon
    White *or* red decorator
    icing

● Prepare dough for Basic Holiday Cookies as directed, *except* substitute peppermint extract or cinnamon oil for the almond extract or coconut flavoring.

● For each cookie, shape about *1 tablespoon* of the dough into a 4x½-inch log. Place logs 2 inches apart on an ungreased cookie sheet. Then shape logs into candy canes. Slightly flatten. Bake in a 325° oven about 15 minutes or till edges are firm and bottoms are very lightly browned. Cool on cookie sheet for 1 minute. Then remove cookies and cool on a wire rack.

● To decorate, use decorator icing and pipe diagonal lines on top of cookies. Makes about 30.

Nutrition information per frosted cookie: 91 calories, 1 g protein, 11 g carbohydrate, 5 g fat, 9 mg cholesterol, 56 mg sodium, 11 mg potassium.

# Sugar Bells

*Celebrate ringing out the old and ringing in the new by serving these crispy cookie bells. (Pictured on pages 66–67.)*

1 recipe Basic Holiday
    Cookies (see page 66)
    Red *or* green colored sugar
    Candy-coated peanuts
    *or* candy-coated milk
    chocolate pieces

● Prepare dough for Holiday Cookies as directed, *except* do not tint dough. Shape dough into *two* 6-inch rolls. Then roll *each* dough roll in red or green sugar to coat surface. Wrap in waxed paper or clear plastic wrap. Chill for 2 to 24 hours.

● Cut dough into ¼-inch-thick slices. Place 1 inch apart on an ungreased cookie sheet. Place a candy-coated peanut or milk chocolate piece on the bottom half of *each* slice for bell clapper. Then let dough slices stand for 1 to 2 minutes to soften for easier handling. Fold in sides of each slice. Pinch in sides to resemble bell shape. Bake and cool as directed. Makes about 48.

Nutrition information per cookie: 66 calories, 1 g protein, 8 g carbohydrate, 3 g fat, 6 mg cholesterol, 35 mg sodium, 6 mg potassium.

# Florentine Triangles

*Candied cherries and pineapple top a rich cookie crust. (Pictured on pages 66–67.)*

1 recipe Basic Holiday
    Cookies (see page 66)
⅓ cup sugar
½ of a 5-ounce can (⅓ cup)
    evaporated milk
¼ cup margarine *or* butter
1 cup coarsely chopped
    candied red and green
    cherries*
½ cup coarsely chopped
    candied pineapple*
¾ cup sliced almonds
2 teaspoons finely shredded
    orange peel
    Powdered sugar (optional)

● For crust, prepare dough for Basic Holiday Cookies as directed, *except* do not tint dough. Pat dough into a lightly greased 13x9x2-inch baking pan. Bake in a 375° oven about 15 minutes or till firm and lightly browned.

● Meanwhile, for fruit mixture, in a medium saucepan combine the sugar, evaporated milk, and margarine or butter. Bring to boiling. Then boil for 1 minute, stirring constantly. Remove from heat. Add cherries, pineapple, almonds, and orange peel. Gently stir till completely coated.

● Spread fruit mixture on top of the baked crust. Bake in the 375° oven for 15 to 18 minutes more or till top is golden. Cool in pan on a wire rack. If desired, sift powdered sugar over top. Cut into triangle-shaped bars. Makes 24.

Nutrition information per bar: 187 calories, 2 g protein, 24 g carbohydrate, 10 g fat, 12 mg cholesterol, 97 mg sodium, 98 mg potassium.

* 1½ cups of *candied mixed fruits and peels* can be substituted for the candied cherries and pineapple.

# Holiday Checkerboards

*A holiday sliced cookie that easily fits into your busy schedule. Mix and form the cookie-dough rolls now, then store them in your freezer and bake them later. (Pictured on pages 66–67.)*

1 recipe Basic Holiday
    Cookies (see page 66)
¼ teaspoon red food coloring
¼ teaspoon green food
    coloring

● Prepare dough for Basic Holiday Cookies as directed, *except* divide the dough in half. To *1 portion*, knead in the red food coloring. To remaining portion, knead in green food coloring.

● Shape pink and green doughs *each* into *four* 10-inch-long ropes. For *each* checkerboard roll, place *1 pink rope* next to *1 green rope*, then place a *another green rope* on top of the first pink rope and *another pink rope* on top of the first green *rope*. (You will have *2* checkerboard rolls total.) Wrap each roll in waxed paper or clear plastic wrap. Chill for 2 to 24 hours.

● Cut dough into ¼-inch-thick slices. Place 1 inch apart on an ungreased cookie sheet. Bake; cool as directed. Makes about 80.

Nutrition information per cookie: 31 calories, 0 g protein, 3 g carbohydrate, 2 g fat, 3 mg cholesterol, 21 mg sodium, 4 mg potassium.

# Santa's Whiskers

¾  cup margarine *or* butter
2  cups all-purpose flour
¾  cup sugar
1  tablespoon milk
1  teaspoon vanilla
¾  cup finely chopped candied
    red *or* green cherries
    *or* a combination
⅓  cup finely chopped pecans
¾  cup coconut

● In a bowl beat margarine or butter with an electric mixer on medium to high speed about 30 seconds or till softened. Add about *half* of the flour, the sugar, milk, and vanilla. Beat till thoroughly combined, scraping sides of bowl occasionally. Beat or stir in the remaining flour. Stir in cherries and pecans.

● Shape dough into *two* 8-inch rolls. Then roll *each* dough roll in coconut to coat surface. Wrap in waxed paper or clear plastic wrap. Chill for 4 to 24 hours.

● Cut dough into ¼-inch-thick slices. Place 1 inch apart on an ungreased cookie sheet. Bake in a 375° oven for 10 to 12 minutes or till edges are golden. Remove cookies and cool on a wire rack. Makes about 60.

Nutrition information per cookie: 60 calories, 1 g protein, 8 g carbohydrate, 3 g fat, 0 mg cholesterol, 27 mg sodium, 15 mg potassium.

# Chocolate Mint Creams

*Look for the pastel cream mint kisses at candy shops, department store candy shops, or food gift shops.*

⅔  cup packed brown sugar
⅓  cup margarine *or* butter
1  tablespoon water
1  6-ounce package (1 cup)
    semisweet chocolate
    pieces
1¼  cups all-purpose flour
1  egg
½  teaspoon baking soda
½  to ¾ pound pastel cream
    mint kisses

● In a medium saucepan heat brown sugar, margarine or butter, and water over medium heat just till melted, stirring constantly. Add chocolate pieces. Heat just till chocolate is melted, stirring constantly. Then transfer mixture to a large mixing bowl and let cool for 10 to 15 minutes.

● Add about *half* of the flour, the egg, and baking soda to the chocolate mixture. Beat with an electric mixer till thoroughly combined. Beat or stir in the remaining flour. (Dough will be soft.) Cover and chill for 1 to 24 hours or till easy to handle.

● Shape dough into 1-inch balls. Place 2 inches apart on an ungreased cookie sheet. Bake in a 350° oven for 8 minutes. Immediately, slightly press a mint into the center of *each* partially baked cookie. Then bake in the 350° oven about 2 minutes more or till cookie edges are firm.

● While mints are still warm and soft, use a knife to spread the mints over tops of cookies like frosting. Remove cookies and let stand on a wire rack till mints are set. Makes about 48.

Nutrition information per cookie: 71 calories, 1 g protein, 12 g carbohydrate, 3 g fat, 6 mg cholesterol, 39 mg sodium, 27 mg potassium.

Gift-Giving Cookie Pops

Happy
May Day!

# Gift-Giving Cookie Pops

*Celebrate the first day of May by giving your secret pal a cookie-flowerpot. To make the pot, insert the cookie pops in a block of florist foam set into a decorative flowerpot.*

1 cup margarine *or* butter
1 8-ounce package cream cheese, softened
3½ cups all-purpose flour
2 cups sugar
1 egg
1 teaspoon baking powder
1 teaspoon vanilla
¼ cup small multicolored decorative candies
    Wooden sticks
    Ribbon (optional)

● In a mixing bowl beat margarine or butter and cream cheese with an electric mixer on medium to high speed about 30 seconds or till softened.

● Add about *half* of the flour, the sugar, egg, baking powder, and vanilla to the margarine mixture. Beat till thoroughly combined, scraping sides of bowl occasionally. Then beat or stir in the remaining flour and the decorative candies. Divide dough in half. Cover and chill for 3 to 24 hours or till easy to handle.

● On a lightly floured surface roll *each* portion of dough to ¼-inch thickness. Cut into 2½- to 3½-inch shapes (such as hearts, flowers, or shamrocks). Place 1 inch apart on an ungreased cookie sheet. Tuck a wooden stick under the center of *each* cookie. Press dough down slightly so that the cookie bakes around the stick. Bake in a 375° oven for 8 to 10 minutes or till edges are firm and bottoms are very lightly browned. Carefully, remove cookies and cool on a wire rack. If desired, tie a ribbon around each stick. Makes about 36.

Nutrition information per cookie: 159 calories, 2 g protein, 21 g carbohydrate, 8 g fat, 15 mg cholesterol, 90 mg sodium, 24 mg potassium.

# Cashew Sugar Cookies

*This buttery cookie is a real cookie tray enhancer.*

1¼ cups all-purpose flour
½ cup ground cashews *or* ground almonds
¼ cup sugar
¼ cup packed brown sugar
½ cup butter
    Sugar
    Whole cashews *or* toasted blanched whole almonds

● In a mixing bowl combine flour, ground nuts, ¼ cup sugar, and brown sugar. Then cut in butter till mixture resembles fine crumbs. Form the mixture into a ball and knead till smooth.

● On a lightly floured surface roll dough to ¼-inch thickness. Cut into 1½-inch circles. Place 1 inch apart on an ungreased cookie sheet. Lightly sprinkle with the additional sugar. Then lightly press a whole nut in the center of each cookie. Bake in a 375° oven for 8 to 10 minutes or till lightly browned. Remove and cool on a wire rack. Makes about 42.

Nutrition information per cookie: 60 calories, 1 g protein, 6 g carbohydrate, 4 g fat, 6 mg cholesterol, 23 mg sodium, 25 mg potassium.

# Chocolate Bourbon Bites

*Here's a wonderful ending to a perfect meal—a rich chocolate after-dinner cookie.*

⅓ cup margarine *or* butter
1 cup all-purpose flour
⅓ cup packed brown sugar
3 tablespoons unsweetened cocoa powder
3 tablespoons bourbon
½ cup miniature semisweet chocolate pieces
1 slightly beaten egg white
¾ cup very finely chopped pecans

● In a bowl beat margarine or butter with an electric mixer on medium to high speed about 30 seconds or till softened.

● Add about *half* of the flour, the brown sugar, cocoa, and bourbon to the margarine. Beat till thoroughly combined, scraping sides of bowl occasionally. Then beat or stir in the remaining flour. Stir in chocolate pieces.

● Shape dough into 1-inch balls. Dip balls into egg white, then roll in the chopped pecans. Place 1 inch apart on an ungreased cookie sheet. Bake in a 350° oven for about 12 minutes or till edges are firm (centers will be soft). Cool on cookie sheet for 1 minute. Then remove the cookies and cool on a wire rack. Makes about 30.

Nutrition information per cookie: 82 calories, 1 g protein, 8 g carbohydrate, 5 g fat, 0 mg cholesterol, 30 mg sodium, 39 mg potassium.

# Walnut Twists

*Serve freshly baked, flaky twists anytime. Keep the unbaked twists on hand in a covered container in the freezer, then bake and glaze twists as directed below.*

½ of a 17½-ounce package (1 sheet) frozen puff pastry
Walnut Filling
Powdered Sugar Icing (see recipe, page 29)
Finely chopped walnuts (optional)

● Let pastry stand at room temperature about 20 minutes or till easy to roll. On a lightly floured surface unfold pastry. Roll into a 14-inch square. Using a pastry wheel, cut square in half.

● Spread filling over *1 portion*. Place remaining pastry half on top of filling. Using the fluted pastry wheel, cut dough into seven 14x1-inch strips. Then cut *each* strip crosswise into *quarters.* (You should have 28 pieces.) Twist each piece twice. Place 2 inches apart on an ungreased cookie sheet. Bake in a 400° oven for 12 to 15 minutes or till golden. Remove twists and cool on a wire rack. Drizzle icing over twists. If desired, sprinkle with nuts. Makes 28.

**Walnut Filling:** In a small saucepan combine 1 slightly beaten *egg*, ¾ cup ground *walnuts*, and ¼ cup packed *brown sugar.* Cook and stir over medium heat just till thickened. Cool before using. Makes ⅔ cup.

Nutrition information per frosted cookie: 56 calories, 1 g protein, 8 g carbohydrate, 3 g fat, 9 mg cholesterol, 25 mg sodium, 20 mg potassium.

# Helpful Cookie Hints

Whether your homemade cookies are destined for your own cookie jar or for a friend across the country, you'll want to be sure to store or pack them so that they stay fresh and unbroken. On the next three pages, we give you hints for doing just that, along with tips for creative but easy cookie gifts.

# Helpful Cookie Hints

**Successful Storage Tips**

Mmmm—nothing beats the taste of fresh cookies. Preserve that just-baked freshness by following these simple storage guidelines:

● Before storing, make sure the cookies are *completely* cool. Otherwise, they'll get soft and stick together.

● Always store crisp and soft cookies separately. Use either tightly covered containers or sealed plastic bags to prevent humidity from softening crisp cookies and air from drying out soft cookies.

● Bar cookies can be stored in either a tightly covered container or in their own baking pan. Just be sure to cover the pan *tightly* with plastic wrap or foil.

● If soft cookies have begun to dry out, restore moistness by wrapping a wedge of raw apple or a slice of bread in a piece of waxed paper and placing it in the container with the cookies. Then seal container tightly. Remove the apple wedge or bread slice after 24 hours.

● For short-term storage, store cookies at room temperature for up to 3 days. Cookies with cream cheese or yogurt in their frosting need to be stored in the refrigerator so that the frosting doesn't spoil.

● For long-term storage, freeze baked cookies in freezer containers or plastic bags for up to 12 months. Before serving, thaw the cookies for 10 to 15 minutes at room temperature.

**Gift-Giving Ideas**

To create clever, extra-special cookie gifts, there's only one rule—let your imagination go! Here are just a few ways to package and present your cookies:

● Choose from a variety of containers, such as old-fashioned crocks, baskets, decorative boxes or tins, unique plates or bowls, pretty canisters, sand pails, fancy molds, wooden cutting boards, and colorful bags.

If the container doesn't have a tight-fitting lid, wrap the cookies in plastic wrap or seal them in a plastic bag before placing them in the container.

● Make an inexpensive cookie container by weaving ribbon through the holes of a plastic fruit or vegetable basket that you can get in the supermarket produce department.

● Create a country look by covering the flat metal lid of a large wide-mouth canning jar with a square piece of fabric cut with pinking shears. Secure the fabric onto the jar by screwing on the outer metal ring. If you like, add a little padding to the top by placing a few cotton balls between the fabric and the metal lid.

● Add extra color to your gift by lining the container with colored tissue paper or wrapping the container filled with cookies in colored cellophane.

● If your recipient has a special interest or enjoys a hobby, give an extra little gift with your package.

## Mix Now, Bake Later

Cookie dough, with the exception of a thin batter or meringue-type dough, can be refrigerated or frozen for baking later.

Store the cookie dough in a tightly covered container in the refrigerator for up to 1 week or in the freezer for up to 6 months. Before baking, thaw the frozen dough in the container. If you find that the dough has become too firm to work with, let it stand at room temperature to soften.

Use ribbon or yarn to tie on a fancy key ring, colored pencils, paintbrushes, dried flowers, cookie cutters, small kitchen gadgets, or a bundle of cinnamon sticks. Or, tuck in a package of flavored tea bags or coffee, a package of decorative recipe cards, collector's stamps, a small framed picture, or a paperback book.

● Celebrate the holidays by adding a festive flair to your cookie package.

At Easter, fill a cellophane-grass-stuffed basket with egg- and bunny-shaped cookies. (Use any cutout cookie recipe on pages 56–62 or 73.)

For Christmas, wrap cookies individually in clear plastic wrap. Then tuck them into Christmas stockings.

For a birthday, cut out unbaked cookie dough the size of the birthday card you plan to give. After the dough is baked and cooled, place the card on top of the cookie, then wrap the cookie and the birthday card in clear pastic wrap. (Use any of the cutout cookie recipes on pages 56–62 or 73.)

### Packing and Mailing Cookies

Surprise faraway friends or relatives by sending them a package of homemade cookies through the mail. By following some simple packing tips, you can make sure that your package will reach its destination in good condition.

Choose cookies that travel well. Most bar cookies are good senders, as are soft, moist drop cookies. Frosted and filled cookies are not good choices because the frosting or filling may soften, causing the cookies to stick to one another or to the wrapping. If you want to send cutout cookies, choose those with rounded edges instead of those with points that break off easily.

Find a heavy box for sending cookies. Line it with plastic wrap or foil. Lay down a generous layer of filler such as plastic bubble wrap, foam packing pieces, or crumpled tissue paper, paper towels, waxed paper, or brown paper bags.

Wrap cookies in pairs, back to back, or individually with plastic wrap. Putting the sturdiest cookies on the bottom, place a single layer

of wrapped cookies on top of the base filler. Then top with another layer of filler. Continue layering, ending with plenty of filler (see photo of cutaway box at left). The box should be full enough to prevent shifting of its contents when closed.

Before closing the box, insert a card with the addresses of both the sender and the receiver, in case the box accidentally is torn open.

Tape the box shut with strapping tape containing reinforcing fibers. Masking and cellophane tapes may crack, tear, or pull away from the package, exposing the contents to cold and moisture. Avoid using paper overwraps and string, which may get torn off or caught in automatic equipment.

Address the box and apply transparent tape over the address to keep it from becoming smeared or blurred from moisture or handling. Mark the box "perishable" to encourage careful handling.

## A Special-Delivery Birthday Party

When kids are away at college or grandparents are living alone, share in their birthday celebration by sending them a box filled with cookies, party snacks, beverage mixes, and small gifts. If you have access to a tape recorder or video camera, wish them a special birthday message on tape.

Choose cookies that travel well (see Packing and Mailing Cookies, above). Pack the cookies in a decorative cookie tin or coffee can with a reclosable plastic lid by layering them in the container with waxed paper. Then pack this container in a well-padded heavy box.

In the box, surround the cookie container with small, gift-wrapped packages of instant coffee, flavored tea or cocoa mixes, dried fruit and nut mixes, and nonbreakable gifts.

# Index

*Keep track of your daily nutrition needs by using the information we provide at the end of each recipe. We've analyzed the nutritional content of each recipe serving for you. When a recipe gives an ingredient substitution, we used the first choice in the analysis. And if it makes a range of servings (such as 4 to 6), we used the smallest number. Ingredients listed as optional weren't included in the calculations.*

# Index

If you would like to order any
additional copies of our books, call
1-800-678-2803 or check with
your local bookstore.